GROW
YOUR
Marriage
BY LEAPS &
BOUNDARIES

To Your Success!

Jerry

JERRY L. COOK, PHD, CFLE

GROW YOUR *Marriage* BY LEAPS & BOUNDARIES

JERRY L. COOK, PHD, CFLE

PLAIN SIGHT PUBLISHING
AN IMPRINT OF CEDAR FORT, INC.
SPRINGVILLE, UTAH

DISCLAIMER: This book is designed for educational purposes and cannot guarantee a particular benefit.

ISBN 13: 978-1-4621-1069-8

Published by Plain Sight Publishing, an imprint of Cedar Fort, Inc.
2373 W. 700 S., Springville, UT 84663
Distributed by Cedar Fort, Inc., www.cedarfort.com

LIBRARY OF CONGRESS CATALOGING-IN-PUBLICATION DATA

Cook, Jerry L., 1971- , author.
Grow your marriage by leaps and boundaries / Jerry L. Cook, PhD, CFLE.
  pages cm
Includes bibliographical references.
ISBN 978-1-4621-1069-8 (alk. paper)
1. Marriage. 2. Married people--Psychology. 3. Married people--Conduct of life. 4. Marriage--Religious aspects--Christianity. I. Title.

HQ734.C837 2012
306.81--dc23

                              2012035179

Cover design by Rebecca J. Greenwood
Cover design © 2012 by Lyle Mortimer
Edited and typeset by Emily S. Chambers

Printed in the United States of America

10 9 8 7 6 5 4 3 2 1

Printed on acid-free paper

Acknowledgments

To all couples who believe marriage is a highest priority.
To my sweetheart wife, Sarah. Thank you for believing in me.
Heidi Doxey, thank you for your editing talents.

CONTENTS

CONTENTS

PREFACE

The dream of happiness in marriage is under assault. Marriage is often viewed as old-fashioned, restrictive, and doomed to failure. We focus so much on the fears of marriage and its dissolution that we have lost faith in the strength of marriage. Sadly, when couples focus on the negative, they soon become what they fear.

Throughout this book you will find ways to improve your marriage, dispel some of the myths about marriage, and better understand why some marriages fail while others succeed. You will be provided with a comprehensive and systematic approach to build on the strengths of your marriage and to "be one" by using boundaries as a means for strengthening, healing, and enjoying your relationship. By changing our actions and gaining certain kinds of knowledge and skills, we change our beliefs about our marriage. Our actions determine where we draw boundaries and whether those boundaries include—or exclude—our spouses.

Used appropriately, boundaries can protect your marriage by helping you and your spouse determine what is best for your relationship. Although this book offers several recommendations about what kinds of boundaries to create or maintain within a marriage, the real key is for you and your spouse to identify, create, and maintain a set of boundaries that both of you feel are important for the success of your marriage.

INTRODUCTION

———————

Marriage takes commitment, patience, and practice. These three characteristics are best shown on the altar of experience, time, and even difficulty. It takes a special kind of love to make marriage work, to make it last, and to make it enjoyable over the course of an entire lifetime. When you feel that level of love, you will naturally feel and show greater levels of respect, commitment, appreciation, and admiration to your spouse than anyone else. That is what it means to "be one."

When you feel that level of love, you will naturally feel and show greater levels of respect, commitment, appreciation, and admiration to your spouse than anyone else.

Whether you have a great marriage or one that is causing you heartache, this book is designed to help you create and maintain the marriage you have always wanted. This will be done by following key principles, such as using healing (rather than hurtful) words, adopting a perspective that brings about positive responses, understanding the role of faith and spirituality, and taking accountability for the growth of your relationship.

INTRODUCTION

By the time you have completed this book, you will have learned, pondered, and applied marriage-based principles in a way that will strengthen your marital commitment, hope, trust, and understanding for each other. This book takes you on a multidimensional journey, one that *you* create, revise, and improve upon over time, as you gain more knowledge and experience.

This book is organized into several sections to help you locate what is most important to you and your marriage. It will give you greater power and understanding for what you can do to strengthen your marital resolve, and it will help you and your spouse address important boundaries before they become a "big deal." The first section talks about the value of marriage, and it provides motivation for working toward a more satisfying marriage. Next is a section about boundaries in general, which provides a context for future (and more) specific chapters on boundaries. At the end of the book is a review or study guide for those who are pressed for time or want to more speedily repeat the material.

To get the most out of your reading, I have two suggestions. The first is to read sequentially, or page by page. The advantage of this approach is that you will develop a daily habit of thinking about and actively building a foundation for the success of your marriage.

My second suggestion is to read the book based upon your interests or needs. For example, if you or your spouse struggle with differences in how to treat the opposite sex, how to manage your finances, or how to conduct your sex life, you can quickly access the specific chapter that applies to your situation in the table of contents.

Before we move on, I'd like to share with you some fundamental principles that are important for any successful marriage. These principals serve as my own belief system about marriage in general.

The first principle is *Equal Power*. Neither the husband nor wife should try to force his or her spouse into applying the strategies in this book if he or she feels uncomfortable doing so. Most men hate reading books about marriage because when their wives say, "Hey, read this and let's work on our marriage," men really hear, "You're a wimpy failure of a husband, and I don't accept you for what or who you currently are." As a man and a husband myself, and also as a scholar in the area of family studies, I have written this book in a way that takes both genders into account, drawing upon each other's strengths, rather than focusing on weaknesses.

The second principle is to *Focus on Resolving the Conflict and Not the Conflict Itself.* Some books and therapy techniques encourage you to raise your voice, get mad, or let all your anger out, with the idea that you have to be "honest" in order to work things out. In this book, however, you will be shown how to resolve conflict effectively while reducing its impact and expression in your relationship.

Forgiveness is the third principle and applies to forgiving your spouse and yourself for not being perfect. Neither of you are perfect, but working together, you can and will become perfect for each other.

1

Benefits of Marriage

When dealing with boundary challenges, we can sometimes forget why marriage is so important. While your own list for why you are married—or why you stay married—is personal, there is a long list of benefits for individuals, families, and society when couples marry and stay married. Compared to divorced or single-parent families, some of these benefits include longer life expectancies, better health, greater wealth, and an increased sense of well-being. In addition, married couples are more likely to be satisfied with their partner and their sex lives, have higher levels of happiness in life, experience greater levels of emotional support, and have stronger bonds with their children, and they are less likely to experience domestic violence. On a larger community or national level, fewer divorces and more successful marriages correspond to decreases in poverty, reductions in the need for the welfare system, and even a reduction in our carbon footprint (such as pollution and waste) because traditional nuclear families consisting of a married couple and their children typically live in one home rather than spreading out across several homes.

We need to educate ourselves and others about the benefits of being married and why strengthening marriages is vital. There is too much at stake to not do so. This should not be a conservative versus liberal or a democrat versus republican issue. It is important for everyone both on a personal level as well as on a national level. Who wouldn't benefit from living in a society with lower levels of poverty, crime, and conflict? Who wouldn't benefit if couples and families had more satisfying and stable relationships?

Some critics argue that promoting marriage is dangerous. It's true that we should not force people to stay married, particularly those who are in abusive relationships, but we harm many families when we neglect to share the truth about what we really know regarding the institution of marriage. Even critics acknowledge the research, but for the sake of political correctness, they sacrifice what is best for most people. They simply do not want to hurt anyone's feelings by telling them the truth. Other skeptics claim that promoting marriage will impede all of the other social progress that has been made over the last several decades. But if "social progress" means increased crime, depression, anxiety, academic problems, poverty, and domestic violence, then count me out.

Who wouldn't benefit if couples and families had more satisfying and stable relationships?

Of course, there has been a great deal of progress in our society. The recognition of personal liberty, the idea that education is not limited to the social elite, the fact that women can become CEOs of successful corporations, and the truth that an African American has become President of the United States—these things speak of what our country was founded upon, namely the right and freedom to pursue our goals. Truly we have taken two steps forward on our path, but we have surely taken another backward. At a time when we know more about relationships than ever before, the rate of marital dissolution is too high. Perhaps it is time to learn what earlier generations did right so that we can adopt some of the practices they used to create and maintain enduring marriages.

My grandparents lived in a place and time when they were taught to be grateful. They were taught to respect others and that the other person was as important as themselves. They were also taught to save a little for a rainy day. These attitudes have largely been replaced by an overall sense of individualism, self-expression, and entitlement. When I visit with my grandma and try to do her dishes, she is always trying to help, and at the very least she keeps turning off the kitchen faucet (before I want it turned off) because she knows the value of conserving. Just because we may not want the exact kind of life our grandparents had does not mean they had it all wrong. In a time when violence seems to be everywhere and we are experiencing the second-worst economic crisis since the Great Depression, I would suggest that our grandparents had a lot of things right. Indeed, I believe that perhaps the reason my grandparents were so wise was that they went through the Great Depression, and they and their generation learned about what was most important. The question now is, will we learn from our current experiences?

In addition to what the government spends on welfare, individuals and families spend billions of dollars each year on nutritional supplements, medicine (including Prozac), housing costs, credit cards and other debt, illegal drugs, the Internet, cable or satellite TV, sexual materials and experiences, and junk food—all in the pursuit of temporary happiness, or at least to be less depressed. Do we understand that so many of our challenges today are associated with a breakdown in families? Do we realize that so many of the things we seek after are merely substitutes for the real benefits that a stable and satisfying marriage can offer? Do we understand the costs of *not* encouraging strong marriages?

Strengthening your marriage will benefit you, your spouse, and your children for generations to come. But even motivation, desire, and effort are not enough to create or maintain a successful marriage. These kinds of marriages follow certain principles, and if you want to build your marriage, you must follow those same principles and do what people in successful marriages do.

Do we understand that so many of our challenges today are associated with a breakdown in families? Do we understand the costs of not encouraging strong marriages?

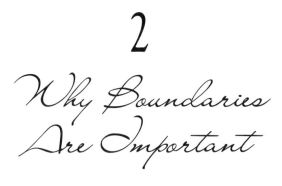

2
Why Boundaries Are Important

Some people looked rather surprised when they found out what this book was about. They asked, "Don't you think people know where that line is? Don't they all know what is right and what is wrong in marriages, but they just choose to cross the line anyway?"

Shortly after writing the first draft of this chapter, I read two tweets on Twitter about how two different couples were struggling with their marriages. For both couples, there was an issue of "emotional infidelity." With at least one of the couples, there was a disagreement about what "flirting" included, and the husband would often focus his time and eyes on pretty women, offering them teasing remarks.

Unfortunately, many couples do *not* know where that line is. Or if they do, they do not know how to establish those boundaries with their spouse. Clear conversations about marital boundaries and how to protect the marriage are rare for many couples. You know you need to love your spouse and "your neighbor," and you know not to commit adultery. Unfortunately, everything between those two spectra is hardly ever discussed, perhaps because we feel that marriage is so sacred or private, or because we assume our spouse has the same values toward marriage that we have. This leaves many couples with more questions than answers. Adultery is over the line, but what else? How do you interact with the opposite sex? How do you talk about finances? Does it matter to you whether a male or female gives you—or your spouse—a gift or a hug? At what precise point do you or the other person first cross that line? Is teasing someone of the opposite sex an example of flirting?

Years ago I read a book by Mary Pipher[1] titled *The Shelter of Each Other: Rebuilding Our Families.* In it she stated that families have always been designed to protect each other from various dangers and that today's families are in particular danger because of societal changes such as increased media, experts who question parental authority, and from peers in a culture that lacks family support and monitoring. My own view is that if we are going to strengthen the family and if children are going to learn how to draw the line between harm and help, then it needs to be first shown by their parents' marriage. They will not learn or accept the need for boundaries if their parents do not know or show by example.

At times we feel that if we even mention the boundaries, we are somehow crossing a line or doing something wrong. It's taboo to be specific when we feel that others are crossing a line with us. But those lines, and knowing how to set them, are vital to the success of any marriage.

When you and your spouse decide *together* where each boundary should be, you work together to make sure each of you are the *only* lover, the *best* friend, and the *most loyal* partner either of you could ever have. Knowing where the boundaries are reduces conflict, increases trust, and can even increase your spirituality.

When you and your spouse decide together where each boundary should be, you work together to make sure each of you are the only lover, the best friend, and the most loyal partner either of you could ever have.

This book addresses several specific boundaries in marriage and explain how each spouse can help bring the marriage closer to perfection. Some of these boundaries involve physical affection, finances, spirituality, social networking, and so on. It's interesting that so much literature on "boundaries" focuses on how to separate yourself from others, including your spouse. While they may be needed in abusive situations, I generally do not feel that encouraging spouses to set boundaries between each other is consistent with Christ's counsel to "be one." I believe that God's commandment to become one is still in effect. For that reason, this book is more about making sure that the most important boundaries are between your marriage and others—and not between you and your spouse.

You may consider some of the strategies or recommendations in this book to be old-fashioned or extreme. Some may be insulted because I write about strong yet subtle temptations that good people experience. Others may think these boundaries are simple common sense. Either way, the reasons for these boundaries will be made clear, and you and your spouse can choose to edit, delete, or revisit these boundaries in a way you feel best fits your marriage and your personal strengths and challenges. Realize that boundaries protect marriages. The more you know about how to create and maintain them, the better off you'll be—whether those boundaries are from this book or ones you and your spouse create and commit to on your own.

You and your spouse can choose to edit, delete, or revisit these boundaries in a way you feel best fits your marriage and your personal strengths and challenges.

Where you draw the line on behalf of your marriage depends on two things. The first is your (and your spouse's) awareness of boundaries and how they can impact your relationship. The second is your sense of motivation or purpose for these boundaries.

Why do so many marriages fail and why do others succeed? The answer to that question likely depends on the people you ask and what their own experiences and observations tell them are the right answers. Some say money; others say sex. While focusing on one conflict over a single issue, like finances or intimacy, is useful for working out concerns with that particular issue, there is really a larger, umbrella-like covering that encompasses so many of the difficulties couples experience.

Dissatisfaction or becoming disenchanted with one's marriage has a lot to do with where couples, individually or collectively, "draw the line" as to what is acceptable, appropriate, or desired in private and public interactions. Sometimes the line *isn't* drawn, and other times it's drawn so far beyond where it should be that a spouse really does not see the end of a marriage until it happens. For others, conflict exists because they cannot agree on how to negotiate boundaries.

Protecting your marriage with boundaries will bring you satisfaction, power, and even greater levels of commitment. Knowing how boundaries impact you and your spouse and knowing how to create healthy boundaries—while limiting harmful boundaries—are essential skills to the stability and success of your marriage.

Pauline Boss,[2] in *Family Stress Management: A Contextual Approach*, notes that ambiguity (or a lack of clear boundaries of who is in or out) in a family often leads to significant stress, and that the knowledge where those boundaries are and being able to defend them is needed to protect that relationship. Boss goes on to explain that daily events and experiences help maintain, or may blur, the boundaries leading to strength or instability. While Boss's points are about a larger family context, it is clear that the marital boundary often determines the strength of the larger family system.

Before we discuss specific boundaries, I'd like you and your spouse to work through an exercise together. Consider the following list of questions about boundaries. Do you already know which boundaries are of particular importance to you and your marriage, or are you unsure? To find out, add one point for each question you answer "yes" to and a zero for each one you answer "no" to. It may be a good idea to mark your numbers on a separate piece of paper or to add them up in your mind. Don't discuss this list with your spouse yet—you will have many opportunities for that soon!

1. Do you and your spouse ever disagree about what to spend your money on?

2. Does either spouse feel nervous about telling the other if they felt a friend or neighbor was flirting with them?

3. Does either spouse feel unappreciated?

4. Is there any tension about the in-laws?

5. Is there any tension about how often one spouse is on social networking sites or other Internet sites, or what TV programs one spouse watches?

6. Are there any disagreements about how to be righteous or unrealistic expectations of perfection?

7. Is there ever tension about your family finances?

8. Does either spouse feel like they need more time and space to be successful in their employment?

9. Is there any frustration about who gets to make the "final decision" on important matters?

10. Does either spouse experience jealousy or envy of the other?

11. Is there any tension about how much time or money either spouse is making for the family?

12. Are there differences in power and influence evident in public or because of different personalities?

13. Does either spouse have difficulty telling the other when they feel hurt by the other?

14. Does either spouse feel like the other spouse is critical or judgmental?

15. Is either spouse negatively influenced by their childhood, or does either one seem to take out childhood frustrations on the other spouse?

16. Is there any tension about how often you have sex or who initiates it?

17. Does either spouse limit the other's social network, personal development, spirituality, or career in any way?

18. Are there disagreements about how to work out conflicts in your marriage?

19. Do you and your spouse have difficulty deciding who should have the final say as a parent with your children?

20. Are there disagreements about how much time and devotion

you ought to give community responsibilities or church assignments?

21. Do you and your spouse disagree about seeing a therapist or an ecclesiastical counselor or about reading books (like this one) on how to improve your marriage?

22. Is there any tension over who gets more sleep?

23. Is there any tension over how long one should attend college, how much to pay for it, or over how much time one ought to invest in education or employment before it "pays off"?

24. Do you disagree about how much money to spend on charity, clothes, or entertainment?

25. Are there any disagreements about what each spouse ought to do with regard to household chores?

26. Is there tension because either spouse does not feel respected or trusted?

How many of the questions above did you or your spouse answer "yes" to? Add up your points and compare your total to your spouses' total. Are they the same or almost the same? Or did one spouse get a score significantly higher or lower than the other? Read on to see what your score means.

0–7   You and your spouse have minimal conflict over boundaries or have not yet had the need to examine your beliefs about boundaries.

8–12   You and your spouse get along most of the time but struggle with some of the boundaries.

13–18   It's likely there are either frequent arguments between you and your spouse or intense fear about talking about boundaries in your marriage.

19–26 You or your spouse or both of you struggle often with boundary creation and maintenance.

The more difficult your marriage is or the greater the potential for conflict, the more likely it is that you and your spouse experience difficulties with boundaries. First though, let's be clear that most couples, if not all, have at least some difficulty with boundaries. Responding "yes" to a certain number of questions does *not* indicate that you are in a bad marriage, nor does your tally determine your odds of finding success in your marriage. Your score only represents the importance of boundaries in your marriage, perhaps at this point in time. Most couples experience a wide range of boundary challenges, at least at some point in their marriage. The success of your marriage has more to do with how you respond to the need for boundaries than the number of boundary challenges you experience.

While boundaries do not eliminate all possible forms of conflict in a marriage, they tend to significantly reduce the need for conflict. Boundaries, whether they are in the form of standards, expectations, or behavior, also serve as mediators or buffers for when things *do* go wrong.

For many couples, the marriage ceremony is an ideal example of how boundaries are formed. For richer or poorer, for better or worse, till death do us part. Vows represent a commitment to show loyalty in everything we do, say, and feel.

Unfortunately, many—perhaps most—married individuals struggle at some time or another with feeling unloved or underappreciated by their spouse, or they have a difficult time talking with their spouse about things they find unrealistic, unfair, or inappropriate. Many couples also struggle with talking about things that may seem important but are taboo. And far too many worry that others will judge their personal worthiness on whether they appear to have a perfect marriage.

While spouses are never perfect, they can be perfect for each other. The process of creating a perfect marriage is one that grows by leaps and through boundary maintenance.

Marriage enters the danger zone when couples do not know how to identify, negotiate, or clarify boundaries in their relationship.

"Sharing" similar values is often more of a negotiation than a one-time event. For example, many couples initially differ on how their spouse should interact with the opposite sex, but couples can negotiate a boundary in a way that both spouses share—or own—that boundary. Refusing to work toward shared boundaries, standards, and expectations leads to a feeling of being disconnected or one of "separate lives," and is a risk factor for divorce and infidelity. Again, be careful not to overemphasize differences, while underestimating similarities, within your marriage. The goal is *not* to look for differences, but to understand the importance of working together to form boundaries in a marriage.

Everyone—including your spouse—changes. Often over the course of a marriage we do not seem to be the same person as when we got married. And some may feel devastated when they find out that their spouse isn't as perfect as they anticipated.

I wonder how many couples could recite or remember the wording of half of the vows they made at their marriage ceremony. Sometimes, the longer we are married, the more we focus on what our spouse should offer us, rather than our own commitments. Too often spouses look for ways of separating themselves emotionally or in other ways from the one they pledged their loyalty to, because one or both of them have "changed" in some way. Boundaries seem to separate spouses, rather than unite them, at least when they are set inappropriately.

In my professional and personal life I have read substantial research and have learned from couples who are successful and from those who have struggled or have divorced. I am convinced that boundary formation and maintenance, including what is allowed in their marriage and what is not, is of greater importance than any specific or single issue couples have conflict over. In truth, the formation, maintenance, and negotiation of boundaries cover most of the challenges that couples experience. This book is designed to give you the tools, words, and strategies you need to create and maintain healthy boundaries.

WHAT ARE BOUNDARIES?

Boundaries are anything that creates space or distance between two (or more) people. When created correctly, they also "draw the line" between right and wrong. Boundaries protect and clarify a couple's purpose, while limiting the influence of anything (or anyone) who could put their marriage in danger. Knowing how to create, maintain, and strengthen marriage boundaries—the way God would want us to—is essential for our happiness.

Boundaries are often found in the form of expectations for one's marriage. Having high expectations can be good for your marriage. Those who have high expectations for their marriage will work harder—and longer—to make certain that those expectations become reality. Indeed, the increased divorce rate in our country may be an outcome of so many couples having low expectations toward the stability of their marriage.

On the other hand, this doesn't mean that we should expect our spouse or our marriage to create 100 percent happiness in our lives. Drs. Whitehead and Popenoe echo this concern in their finding that over 90 percent of couples marry with the expectation that their spouse will fully complement—or complete—them, their lives, and their happiness.[3] In other words, most individuals marry thinking that the other person will make their lives better, happier, and easier in every way—rather than accepting personal responsibility for making their life and marriage great.

Boundaries protect and clarify a couple's purpose, while limiting the influence of anything (or anyone) who could put their marriage in danger.

The truth is that boundaries are set in our minds before they're set in our marriage. How we think about something determines how we will act—or react—to certain situations, behaviors, and challenges. Ironically, we all recognize that we need to have faith before we can see miracles in our lives, yet too often we ask God for a great marriage before we have the confidence and works that can lead to one.

Proper boundaries serve as our moral "smoke detectors," letting us know when there is danger. But just like smoke detectors, boundaries need to be checked, maintained, and placed correctly to be most effective. If you've ever had a smoke detector that was oversensitive or didn't work even when the house was filled with smoke, you know that lack of detection or a "false negative" in detecting smoke to be annoying at best, and very dangerous at worst.

Drawing boundaries, and knowing where those boundaries are, allows them to serve as guides in our marriage. One way that boundaries are formed is through the expectations or standards that each spouse has for their marriage, themselves, and their spouse. The higher and more clear the standards are in a marriage, the more clear the boundary is. These expectations or standards can involve communicating with each other, physical affection, and the emotional investment each spouse makes.

Once the boundaries are set, it's clear when we have passed them.

When my daughter was five years old, she and I were in the car and at an intersection whose light would only stay green for a few seconds. This led to a long line and wait time. Several green lights had come and gone, but we were still waiting. Finally, I sensed an opportunity! A green light came and two vehicles went through. I knew I'd never make it on a green, but I floored it to make it through before the light turned red. I made it and was feeling pretty proud of myself until my daughter exclaimed, "Daddy! You went through a yellow light!" I explained to her that it was illegal to go through a red, but that it was okay to go through a yellow if you had to. She then taught me a wonderful lesson. "But, Daddy, that light was yellow and instead of slowing down, you sped up."

It's interesting how so many couples understand that they are not to go into or through something they know is completely wrong (like having an affair), but many of these same couples are unaware of the cautions or yellow lights that quickly escalate into inappropriate feelings for others or a decreased commitment for their spouse. The moment you start rationalizing or overlooking the importance of those warning signals is the moment you jeopardize your marriage. The distance between a yellow light and a red light is quite small and happens more quickly than most people anticipate.

Just like having a driver's license does not insure individuals from a crash, being married, or having a marriage license, is no guarantee for safety for a couple's relationship. Going over the line will ultimately cause heartache to someone, regardless of the licensed person's ability, history, or intent.

Boundaries serve as the rules that determine how spouses treat each other, and they define what roles each is to fulfill, whether it be how many hours one spouse is employed or who is supposed to take out the trash that week. From how you're expected to treat each other to how you should or shouldn't interact with others, the clarity of your marital boundaries serves as a guide for your future together.

Have you or anyone you know ever said one of the following?

- "I wish my husband would just treat me better. Can't he just do that?"
- "We've been married for ten years. You'd think she'd figure out what I need."
- "If he really loves me, he'd figure out what he needs to do better."
- "I've given all my heart to her, and what do I get in return? She doesn't get it."

These statements reflect not only the need for boundaries, but the fact that few couples understand what each other's boundaries are. Instead they expect that their spouses are playing by the exact same rules they are. Even when couples use the same words, that doesn't guarantee that both people are thinking the same thing. A silly memory about language barriers may illustrate this point.

Years ago my wife and I were working for a temporary employment agency, and we were called to go work for a popular exercise equipment company. Over the telephone, the agency told us to dress casually. They said that we would be testing the resistance of new exercise equipment. We were told we'd have a lot of fun doing this and that there would probably be music. We loved the idea—getting paid to exercise! When we got there, we were told we needed to go onto the assembly line. We told the supervisor that wasn't what we were asked to do. We were here to work out on the exercise equipment and test their capabilities. The supervisor said, "Exactly," in a patronizing voice. "You are to work on the assembly line, and for each piece that comes across, you move the dial like so, and the gadget like so, testing the equipment's capacities." There may have been music but the machinery was so loud, we couldn't hear it.

Despite major advances in medicine, technology, and other things, we still haven't found a way to perfectly read minds—even when the mind is our spouse's. It sounds silly, doesn't it? And yet when we get offended or hurt, that's the exact excuse we come up with. "If my spouse really loved me . . ."

Whether you have a great marriage and want it to become better, or you and your spouse are having several problems in your marriage, this book will help you (1) identify the boundaries that currently exist in your marriage and (2) understand how to create boundaries in a way that will strengthen your marriage, rather than bring it down. This book will also help you if you struggle with jealousy or pain from being hurt, or if you have had your trust in your loved one challenged. Its purpose is to enable you to successfully negotiate boundaries with your spouse.

Regardless of your situation, know that God is mindful of you and your marriage. He wants to bless your relationship and your efforts. Make sure you draw the line with Him on your side at all times. In each chapter, I offer recommendations on what healthy boundaries need to be created and what damaging boundaries need to be repaired. *Please consider them as "recommendations," and prayerfully consider with your spouse and God what your marriage needs.* You and your spouse may want to focus on some boundaries for now and revise or let others go, based upon how you each feel about them. Most important, do not make an issue out of something that does not exist! This book is *not* about finding problems in your spouse; it's about learning how to negotiate where those boundaries should be.

Here are my recommendations for you as you read this book:

Keep an open mind. Whether you agree with the comments in

this book or not, realize that your spouse has had different experiences with boundaries. At some point your spouse will have a different perception than you do. Our experiences shape our values, so try not to be judgmental of your spouse when opinions differ. As you set boundaries with your spouse, keep in mind the underlying purpose of having boundaries, rather than simply agreeing to a mutual checklist of what you will or won't do.

This book is more about increasing marital cohesion than compulsory marital improvements.

If discussing a certain issue with your spouse is too confrontational, painful, or frustrating for either of you, you should strongly consider moving to another topic or goal that both of you agree is more manageable. While eliminating conflicts is a worthy goal, it's even more important that your marriage experiences more successes than challenges.

Selecting what words to say about boundaries is as important as the boundaries themselves.

Be honest and willing to listen—without judgment. It is relatively common for one spouse to give in to the other when there is a disagreement about how to create and enforce boundaries. But ideally each person's voice should be valued, heard, and respected.

Consider writing your boundaries down, including why they are meaningful to your marriage, and frequently review your list to see if you and your spouse need to revise it.

Recognize that we are all imperfect. The bigger the changes in your boundaries, the harder it will be to change your behavior. Believe in yourself, your spouse, and your marriage, but also believe in each of these enough to be able to forgive when forgiveness is needed.

NOTES

1. Mary Pipher, *The Shelter of Each Other: Rebuilding our Families* (New York: Balletine Books, 1996), 10–14.

2. Pauline Boss, *Family Stress Management: A Contextual Approach* 2nd edition (Thousand Oaks, CA: Sage, 2002), 95–97.

3. Whitehead, B., & Popenoe, D., *The State of Our Unions: The social*

health of marriage in America (New Brunswick, NJ: Rutgers University, National Marriage Project, 2001).

3

Physical Boundaries

I still remember the first time Sarah (now my wife) kissed me in public. It was the first time anyone (aside from my mother!) had ever kissed me in public. Showing affection in public not only made my heart race, it also told me, "This affection is for you and only you, and I'm not afraid to show it."

Physical boundaries are usually the most recognizable boundaries, because they are boundaries you can see. They can also be the first boundaries that signal to spouses that they are not getting along, or on the extreme end, that they are no longer "compatible." Couples who are not getting along draw more rigid boundaries within their marriage relationship, or between the spouses. When you get angry with your spouse, you "draw the line" or create a boundary between you and your spouse by essentially (or directly saying), "I no longer feel as close to you." Hugs, kisses, sex, and positive words become less common, which often extends the line or boundary farther away from one's marriage.

How often affection is given, whether it is given in public or private, and to whom it is given serve as powerful boundaries. The more voluntary affection within the couple, the smaller the boundary is between the spouses. You and your spouse will want to be clear about what affection means to each of you, including how it is given within the marriage and how it is given to those outside your marriage. Are you or your spouse jealous or angry about how much affection one of you gives to friends or—especially—to the opposite sex? Jealousy or anger develops because of the perception that one spouse has crossed the line and blurred the boundary between what—and who—should be most important. The other spouse then feels that their marriage and personal value is under attack.

Often this affection leads to defensiveness. For example, if a wife shows more affection for other men than her husband feels is appropriate, he'll feel threatened. This will lead him to say something about his anger or pain. The wife will then feel defensive and say something like, "What you don't trust me? I'm your wife!" In turn, another boundary is placed *between* these two, with neither spouse feeling loved or respected.

In the Old Testament, God commanded Adam and Eve to "be one." The larger the boundaries between them, the less they could fulfill that commandment. However, being one has more to do with how spouses address differences than whether those differences exist in the first place. Being one means treating your spouse the way you would want to be treated.

Different cultural backgrounds, personalities (such as extrovert versus introvert), family experiences, and past abuse can influence how and where each spouse feels that boundaries—both between the spouses and between others—ought to be placed. This is perhaps most evident in the affection boundary. Some people feel quite comfortable with talking and enjoying the opposite sex's company, while others see it as an affront to their marriage. Others see certain kinds of affection as something to be shared only between spouses, so when their spouses share it with others it makes them feel as if they and their marriages are less valued.

After discussing your beliefs about what affection means, when it ought to be given to each other, and when it can appropriately be given to others, consider in what ways you can change your behavior so that it does not impact your marriage. This will require examining the underlying reasons behind your behavior. For example, if your spouse is uncomfortable with you hugging someone of the opposite sex, is it because you are showing less affection to your spouse or is it because your spouse perceives you as being less committed to the relationship, or could it be a combination of the two? Or if you are frequently jealous of your spouse's affection to others, consider that you might be living a double standard; ask yourself if you trust your spouse, or think about how you could perhaps decrease your spouse's affection for others by doing more things that would make your spouse want to be affectionate with you.

The answers for identifying, clarifying, and repairing boundaries are anything but simple, and it is quite difficult to not become judgmental or hurt when you feel that certain behaviors, feelings, or thoughts ought to be reserved for you and you only. It is also difficult if you want to socialize but feel judged by your spouse for doing so. But with your commitment to do what's right for your marriage, and with your spouse's commitment, you will find great success.

As we discussed in the last chapter, selecting what words to say about boundaries is as important as the boundaries themselves. In reality, the words we use *are* boundaries. Let's look at the following example of a fictional couple who has different perceptions and values about physical affection with others.

Wife: You don't love me.
Husband: What are you even talking about?

Obviously, that didn't go well. Both spouses were focused on themselves and didn't articulate themselves very well. Let's try it again.

Wife: I'm uncomfortable when you give hugs to other women.
Husband: I'm not sure why, honey. I love you, so please don't worry about it.

A little better, but we still have a long way to go. The wife is trying to take ownership of how she feels, but her husband still doesn't understand the intensity or validity of her feelings. Let's try it again.

Wife: Can we talk about something for a minute?

Husband: What's the matter?"

Wife: I'm uncomfortable when you give hugs to other women.

Husband: I'm sorry, honey. I wouldn't want to do anything that hurts you or our relationship.

Much better, right? Both spouses may have felt defensive, but they still tried to be respectful of each other. Let's try once more to see where this can go.

Wife: Hi, honey. Can we take a moment to talk about something in private?

Husband: Definitely. What would you like to talk about?

Wife: For awhile now I have felt uncomfortable when you and other women hug.

Husband: I'm sorry, love. I wouldn't want anything to come between us or our marriage.

Wife: Neither would I.

Husband: It might be awkward to bring it up, but I may need some help knowing when you feel uncomfortable. Can you give me some examples?

Wife: At the party at the Jensons' last night, it seemed like you often touched women on their arms.

Husband: It's the frequent touching that makes you feel uncomfortable.

Wife: Yes.

Husband: I actually never thought about that. I grew up with several sisters and that's just how we communicated. I never thought it meant anything. But I can see that it does to you.

In this example, each spouse tried to show appreciation for the other during a difficult conversation. This was done first by asking whether it would be okay to discuss something and then by validating the marriage as being more important than other relationships. This largely dispelled any feelings of defensiveness, allowing them to openly discuss what affection meant to them. Each spouse avoided being critical of the other. The husband could have said, "Touching is not the same as a hug." And the wife could have said, "You may have learned to be that way with your sisters, but that doesn't give you an excuse to be that way with others."

Talking about sensitive issues takes time, practice, trust, and empathy.

Proximity is another physical boundary. It has to do with how much space or distance can be seen between you and your spouse. For example, when one spouse is away at work and the other is not, their proximity is greater. While proximity often refers to longer distances, I like to think of it in another application, namely how much physical space—inches or feet—is between you and your spouse. Do you generally sit together, how close are your bodies and faces, and how close are the two of you when one person is interacting with the opposite sex?

My wife and I love to watch two couples in our ward, one is middle-aged and the other is "up there" in age. Both couples always sit by each other, compliment each other, and look comfortable with their spouses.

Proximity is similar to "affection" because typically the closer one sits, leans into, or moves one's body toward the person he or she is talking with, the closer those two people feel. I have seen some couples who seldom talk to people of the opposite sex, while others will not talk with the opposite sex unless their spouse is present. I have also seen those who continually show affection to their spouses even when one is doing all the talking with someone of the opposite sex. And I have seen those who limit their time with their spouse and spend much of their time with members of the opposite sex. Obviously there is great variation in how comfortable people are with their proximity to others.

Similarly, friends and colleagues of mine have told me they are uncomfortable with the growing trend for opposite sex coworkers (in employment and church circles) who are not married to each other to travel together for meetings or other business purposes.

One colleague said, "It used to be a big deal while I was growing up—it was definitely against the standard to be in the car with someone of the opposite sex whom you were not married to unless your spouse was with you."

I know a young couple that I love to watch together. They do not yet have any children. She is busy pursuing a medical degree, and he has finished his bachelor's degree and recently obtained a managerial position. I enjoy watching them because when they are alone, they typically only converse with members of the same sex. When they are together, they are comfortable talking with the opposite sex. They are both competent and confident, but they are sensitive to each other's need for proximity and affection. Their marriage is growing by leaps and boundaries.

They are sensitive to each other's need for proximity and affection. Their marriage is growing by leaps and boundaries.

On the other hand, we need to be careful, whether it's with affection or proximity, that we do not smother our spouse and that we do not feel smothered ourselves. There may be times when certain couples agree that an adjustment in your proximity boundaries is appropriate. For example, some people need more time to be alone after an argument; others air their grievances and feel better right away. Even without an argument, it's not wrong to want some alone time, a breather, or hobbies or interests you call your own. The key with individual interests is to make them a piece of your life and not what defines your marriage.

It's important for women to understand that close physical proximity and contact with men will make most men feel something—whether it is romantic, sensual, or exciting in nature. Those feelings of interest or romance will intensify as the distance becomes closer or touching becomes more common, personal, or comforting. The movement of a feminine hand in a circular motion on a man's back or neck can powerfully alter the man's mood, yet I have seen women do this just to get a man's attention. (She definitely will have his attention after that.) I have been in several groups of men where they have talked about supposedly innocent exchanges or interactions, but the men admit to experiencing more intense feelings about the woman, even though all she is offering is a simple compliment or conversation. Many men fight these feelings, but it's clear they are common among men, regardless of their marital, socioeconomic, or even religious status.

I have also observed that males tend to be more likely to increase their proximity and affection to females who appear vulnerable or dependent on them. Many men like to feel like they are rescuing women and they like to solve women's problems, whether those women are married to them or not. How much of this is purely biological and how much is due to social pressures is not clear, but the way in which women talk about their circumstances, particularly if they sound or act like they or their husbands are helpless, can affect the chance that other men will cross that line of protection and perhaps some accompanying boundaries they should not cross.

Deborah Tannen, in her landmark book *You Just Don't Understand*, notes that men will seek to solve problems for attractive women because they believe consciously or otherwise that the women will become drawn to them.[1] Ironically, women may not see a man solving their problems as a romantic or sensual gesture, but chances are high that a man who is rescuing a woman will feel that way. I believe this is one reason why pornography can be so dangerous to a marriage. Women are depicted as eager, interested, vulnerable, and, from the male's perspective, unable to criticize him.

Willard Harley, in *His Needs, Her Needs: Building an Affair-Proof Marriage*, goes even further by stating that the primary need for men in their marriage is sexual fulfillment, and that the primary needs for women in their marriage are affection and conversation. He further clarifies that an affair usually begins where two people are just friends but become the catalysts for fulfilling each other's needs, rather than obtaining them from their own marriage.[2]

An affectionate female friend once joked that she wished I would teach her husband how to be a good husband. Even though she was teasing, I could tell she wasn't happy with her husband. A week after she made the comment to me, another man came up from behind the woman, put both of his arms around the woman's neck and massaged her shoulders, asking, "Have you seen my wife?" The two were not married, and she looked terrified. I wondered who else she had shared her concern about her husband with.

Most of the time, simple exchanges of attention are nothing more than an expression of the fact that two people are enjoying a conversation about something they are interested in. However, if, as a woman, you touch a man's neck, arm, or leg, be prepared for the possibility that he may think you are interested in him. It doesn't matter if this effect is biologically based or if it's because men's brains have been saturated with false images as to what respect and love is from the media. What you should consider is the real effect it has on many men.

Men, if you find yourself attracted to someone you are not married to, even if there was no intent or desire to flirt, leave immediately! The same applies for women who get the impression that another man is attracted to them. Ladies, do not sell yourself short by thinking that you are not beautiful enough to flirt with. Regardless of your height, weight, or outward appearance, it can happen. It does happen. And assuming it could never happen with any man or woman is inviting disaster. Many marriages have been destroyed when spouses justify their interactions with people outside their marriages because it "feels good," they feel wanted, or they even feel that they deserve the affection or admiration of another who is not their spouse.

In an interesting twist on physical boundaries, Jerry Jenkins, author of *Hedges,* shares his belief that men are unable to conquer lust, at least in this lifetime. His argument is that men are given strong urges, and that these are designed by God. He continues to warn that when men are confronted with sexual attraction in any form, they are commanded to flee, to get out, and to run.[3]

Let's also state the obvious: women can be attracted to other men, even though it typically does not happen as quickly as men's patterns of attraction. While a man's good looks serve as part of the attraction, it also tends to occur when a woman feels that a man is highly respected by others, is popular, or takes an exceptional interest in her by listening to her. Do not compromise who you are affectionate with or spend time with someone who is not your spouse just because you do not feel any sexual feelings for a certain person. Again, if you feel emotionally close to a man or if you seek out his attention, I'm willing to bet his thoughts are light years ahead of yours. Most affairs begin with emotional needs being met by another person, not necessarily by having sex. They begin with one person finding someone of the opposite sex who "gets" them or who listens to them, and then both people continue to pursue or accept those emotional encounters.

Stress, fatigue, illness, and memories can all have an impact on one's perception and interest in sex and affection. A low self-esteem may reduce or increase that interest. Proper nutrition, exercise, relaxation, or counseling and medication may need to be considered.

Men, trust that your wife is more likely to know when a woman is interested in you. Women, trust your husband if he says he has noticed another man crossing that line. Learn the language that will let you tell your spouse this in a way that will not accuse them. We were all more sensitive about what strategies, techniques, and even feelings attracted us to members of the opposite sex before marriage. Use those skills now to help you know when a boundary has been crossed.

If you sense something inappropriate in a conversation or interaction between your spouse and a member of the opposite sex, show consideration for your spouse by getting closer to him or her. Leaning into, holding, touching, and making eye contact with each other can all indicate to an outside party that you are committed to one another. Consider making up a code word that only you and your spouse know to signify that it's time to terminate a conversation while it's occurring. In an emergency, you may even consider going up to your spouse and rehearsing your marital vows in front of the other person. Or if the line has seriously been crossed, ask the offender what their marriage means to them.

It may seem taboo to discuss—let alone acknowledge—that we and our spouses can be attracted to others. It can even be painful. But understanding—although not flaunting—those attractions is necessary if you want to create healthy boundaries between your marriage and others. I've often heard that "it's okay to look once, but don't look twice" at those you feel attracted to (other than your spouse, of course). Some even joke that you should make that first look as long as possible so that you don't have to look twice. I do not find the humor in this kind of rationalization.

It would be wise to consider David, who had such incredible faith as a child that he relied upon the Lord and delivered all of Israel. Unfortunately, David became so enthralled with the beauty of a woman, and perhaps his own importance, that he committed sins that God hates the most. Perhaps this is why he pleads with his readers to not make the same first mistake of justifying a weakening of marital boundaries. Even that first look or desire can be dangerous if we don't realize its potential consequences until it's too late. David warns, "Lust not after her beauty in thine heart. . . . Can a man take fire his bosom, and his clothes not be burned?" (Proverbs 6: 26–28).

Recognize that it is natural to be attracted to more than one person, but just because it is natural does not mean it is right or healthy. One of the best ways to recognize if you are hearkening to Christ's teachings is if your attraction to your spouse is strong and ever growing while your desire for recognition and admiration from the opposite sex is always lessening. These feelings are something you can choose to have or not. It is within your power and commanded of God that you control them. Even if it's difficult, I know that all things are possible with God's help.

Let's look at another fictional couple. They are having a conversation about proximity boundaries.

Dillon: Sue, I don't get it. You go around flirting with guys. It's seriously annoying.

Sue: No, I guess you don't understand. I like feeling appreciated and pretty, and you never tell me that I'm either one of those.

That's definitely not a good situation. What Sue and Dillon don't know is that each of them is having their own conversation. They assume the other knows what they're feeling, and their words are leading their relationship and the argument into a downward spiral. Let's try again.

Dillon: Sue, I love you, but when you flirt with other guys it really makes me feel like you don't love me.

Sue: Fine, I won't flirt. Okay? Seriously, why do you have to be so controlling?

Clearly this relationship is full of intense feelings, and each person feels threatened and unimportant to the other. Dillon's introductory comment, "I love you, but," is the first red flag. He may be trying to give appreciation, but Sue hears that his love comes with exceptions and caveats. This tells her that the game of love is to be played by his rules only. Sue is defensive. She plays the martyr but doesn't really understand the situation or her husband's concern. She then throws in a final dig by telling him he's controlling. It's likely that this issue has come up before and she evidently feels a lack of autonomy over her feelings and behaviors, which causes her to strike back. No matter what Dillon says next, he'll be viewed as an abusive spouse.

What could remedy this conflict? Let's see how it might be done.

Dillon: Sue, can we visit for a few minutes about something that I think is hurting our relationship?

Sue: You think I'm flirting with other guys again, right?

Dillon: I know I haven't said the right words in the past, and I apologize for that. You probably think that I'm controlling. I don't want to be. I really love you and want you to know that our marriage is the most important relationship to me. That's why I feel so threatened when you lean into guys or when you move away from me to laugh at things they say. I feel threatened, and I feel like our marriage is threatened.

Sue: Thanks for sharing that, Dillon. I guess I hadn't thought of it like that before. Can you give me some examples of when you think I'm flirting with other guys? I just thought you didn't want me to be around any guys at all.

Dillon: Maybe "flirting" wasn't the right word. . .

Sue: But you feel it's inappropriate?

Dillon: I really feel like less of a man when you spend so much time with guys and when you laugh at other guys' jokes and not mine. I kind of feel paralyzed when I see you touching other guys' arms.

Sue: You feel that I value other guys' ideas more than yours.

Dillon: Yeah, I guess that's part of it. When you laugh at my jokes or when you touch my arm, I feel like I'm the only one for you. And when you do it more with other guys, then I think they feel that way too. I thought maybe you felt the same.

Sue: Wow, I really never knew that. I think I just do those things when I'm trying to connect with people—I didn't really think that was how you or another guy might think about it. Would it help if . . . ?

This was a great example. Both spouses generally valued their relationship enough to ward off any confrontation, jealousy, or animosity that could arise from this interaction. Dillon deflected Sue's initial defensiveness ("You think I'm flirting with other guys again, right?") by accepting responsibility for his part in the conflict. Then he validated how unconditionally important she was to him. Sue stated her appreciation for the fact that Dillon shared his thoughts and feelings. She was willing to continue to examine her own behavior, even after Dillon appeared to be letting the whole issue go by saying, "Maybe flirting isn't the right word." Sue and Dillon were able to discuss an awkward subject because each person showed respect for the other's feelings and perceptions.

Of course, many times the boundaries aren't always so smoothly formed and the process requires more give and take. Consider if Sue and Dillon had started off the same way, but eventually traveled to a different route.

Dillon: Sue, can we visit for a few minutes about something that I think is hurting our relationship?

Sue: You think I'm flirting again with other guys, right?

Dillon: I know I haven't said the right words in the past, and I apologize for that. You probably think that I'm controlling. I don't want to be. I really love you and want you to know that our marriage is the most important relationship to me. That's why I feel so threatened when you lean into guys, or when they stand so close to you. I feel threatened, and I feel like our marriage is threatened.

Sue: Thanks for sharing that, Dillon. I guess I hadn't thought of it like that before. Can you give me some examples of when you think I'm flirting with other guys? I just thought you didn't want me to be around any guys at all.

Dillon: Maybe "flirting" wasn't the right word . . .

Sue: But you feel it's inappropriate?

Dillon: I really feel like less of a man when you laugh at other guys' jokes and not mine. I kinda feel paralyzed when I see you touching other guys' arms.

Sue: You feel that I value other guys' ideas more than yours.

Dillon: Yeah, I guess that's part of it. When you laugh at my jokes or when you touch my arm, I feel like I'm the only one for you. And when you do it more with other guys, then I think they feel the same way.

Sue: I hadn't really thought of it that way. Dillon, I want you to know you're the only one for me, but I feel like I'd be dishonest if I said I could just stop being affectionate. I've been this way for a long time. Is there anything I or we can do that will still help?

Dillon: I don't know . . .

Sue: Honey, please know that I love you, and you are the only one for me. How about this: when you feel I am being too affectionate with others you can come up and hug me or squeeze my hand. That'll be a sign for me to back off and give you more affection.

Dillon: I think I could live with those changes. I love you too, Sue.

This situation worked well because both spouses were willing to negotiate where the boundary was. Both were sensitive to each other and affirmed that they loved each other. Again, every individual and couple is different, and you'll want to allow for some creativity with how you define the boundaries in your marriage.

I have several rules about boundaries for myself, which I use to protect my heart, mind, and marriage. I personally avoid being in the house if we have hired help cleaning the house and my wife is gone, since they have always been females thus far. Typically my wife tries to schedule the help for when she will be home. Similarly,

I try to avoid entering a house if the wife is home and the husband is not. Even if nothing happens, appearances or false accusations are too complicated, and it's not anything I'd want to be involved with. Playdates for our children can also be awkward at times. Usually the parent (me) is invited into the house, even if only the mom is home. I'm very involved with my children's lives and activities, and it isn't uncommon for a mother to bring her own children over to play while I am home but my wife is not. When a mother wants to talk with me, I am comfortable conversing with her but try to keep much of the conversation focused on my wife's positive qualities or on the kids. I also don't mind questions about my work, but I always keep a distance of at least three feet or more.

It isn't uncommon for a man to come to the door to discuss payment for yard work with my wife. I personally do not have a problem with this if the man keeps it professional, but if there is more chit-chat than actual work, I am not comfortable.

Again, everyone has a different comfort level. It doesn't please me to say this, but I simply don't trust myself. I don't want to find out what I would do if I was tempted. It's not worth it. I stay as far from that temptation as possible because I have seen so many good people fall when they did not place boundaries where they should have been. Call me old-fashioned, but I want my wife to know I value my covenants with her more than I value those other interactions.

I've also been in some social situations when men have come up to me and the first words out of their mouth were "Where's your wife?" Then they would walk away when they got their answer. My wife is beautiful. I know it and so do they. And I'm okay with that, as long as they know that I'll do anything to protect our marriage, and that if they ever said or did something (even for the sake of comedy) that impacted my marriage, that friendship would be done. Regardless of romantic intentions or a lack thereof, there is danger when someone of your gender is more focused on your spouse than on making conversation with you. Don't overlook this warning signal. While their question might be completely innocent, be sure you know where their focus is and where it ought to be.

If you want to change your boundaries of affection and

proximity, you can. Start by avoiding justifications or rationalizations about inappropriate behavior. Don't use excuses like, "That's just the way I am" or "This is how God made me." God also made you to understand right from wrong, and God has given you the power to change.

This isn't to minimize how hard it can be to change the amount of affection we give to others and how much we accept from others. You just need to understand that it can be done. Another helpful suggestion is to ask your spouse to role-play with you so that you can both be alerted to the new boundaries you are trying to put in place. Be patient with yourself and your spouse if this is something you want to change. When people are used to you being affectionate, they are drawn to you for that reason. People will continue to seek your attention, for better or worse, until you give them reason not to.

If you want to reserve more of your affection for your spouse, then you need to prepare to take a stand. When someone of the opposite sex comes up to you and you sense they will break your personal boundary (however you define it), extend your hand out and grab theirs, if necessary, to shake it. If they still try to get closer, this is a definite sign that they are not respectful of your boundaries or your marriage. Tell them that hugs are reserved for your spouse. If they give you affection you want reserved for your spouse, you need to take a stand and tell them not to do so or else the behavior is likely to be repeated. Just because a boundary is clear to you does not mean that it is clear to others.

If you want to reserve more of your affection for your spouse, then you need to prepare to take a stand.

If you anticipate that someone who is too "handsy" wants to touch you, put your hand out straight as you stand back. The hand will help break the barrier and create a new physical boundary. Keep your arm strong and straight. You may also choose to enforce the boundary with them by pretending you are a traffic cop and telling someone to stop. Practice what you would do or say if you were introducing yourself, if the two of you were becoming reacquainted, or if you were discussing something you are passionate about. Use the hand motion for "stop" while you are talking if someone crosses the line. If you want to be more subtle, wave "hello" by extending your hand, with wrist slightly back, and taking a step back if the person gets closer than your comfort level. This creates a powerful nonverbal boundary. Or if you know you will be around this type of person, you can try to arrange to have your spouse with you. This will be comforting for both of you.

Sometimes not looking at people will also let them know you are not interested in talking with them. Regardless of your strategy, if others do not respect your boundary, you always have the right to leave, tell them to let go, tell someone else what is going on, or file a complaint of sexual harassment if it happens at work.

This is really self-defense for the marriage. My wife, Sarah, and I practiced these strategies, and when I tried to surprise her with a hug, she put both of her arms straight out and gut-checked me. We laughed so hard we could barely stand up straight, but I promised her I would support her and stand by her if she ever did that to anyone who she felt was crossing the line with her. The more you practice it, the more natural it will be. You can actually learn to create these physical boundaries without making a scene if you allow them to become a regular part of how you interact with people you do not trust.

Shortly after Sarah and I practiced these moves together, she went to a conference where she knew there would be several very affectionate people. But she employed these strategies during the conference and came comfortable and confident with being able to maintain boundaries. The scriptures indicate that the true honor of a woman (and I would include a man) is whether they are loyal to their spouse. If so, others will perceive their spouse in the same way that they do (Proverbs 31: 10–12, 23, 25, and 28). Clearly, men will judge other men by how those men are treated by their wives; comparably, how husbands treat their wives will yield the same blessings or problems. A more modern interpretation is given below each verse.

Who can find a virtuous woman? for her price is far above rubies.
When you can find a spouse who knows right from wrong—including where he or she maintains boundaries between right and

wrong and especially a spouse who is extremely faithful to his or her partner—that person is more valuable than any money you can find.

The heart of her husband doth safely trust in her, so that he shall have no need of spoil.

You can always believe in what your spouse says, and you will never need to look elsewhere to have your emotional needs met.

She will do him good and not evil all the days of her life.

When the boundaries are set, there isn't any doubt, and it defines how each person acts with his or her spouse and with others.

Her husband is known in the gates, when he sitteth among the elders of the land.

Your spouse and family will be admired and respected more than if you were just rich with money.

Strength and honour are her clothing; and she shall rejoice in time to come.

Morality is part of each spouse's attire, and each will receive their reward for being so clothed.

Her children arise up, and call her blessed; her husband also, and he praiseth her.

How you treat your spouse will influence how your children see you and your spouse.

PHYSICAL INTIMACY

Jesus clarified and expanded the boundary of sexuality when He explained that even looking upon a non-spouse to lust after that person is a form of adultery. Participating in adultery is wrong and wrecks too many marriages. It often begins with a seemingly innocent look, touch, smile, or thought. We do not always know where that thought or emotion will lead. Do not assume that just because you have not had sex with someone other than your spouse that you have fully lived your marital vows. If you have emotionally sought out someone else or have tolerated someone lusting after you in any way, you have also crossed that line.

Sex serves as a boundary that not only strengthens a marriage, but defines the relationship as something of greater value. In general, couples who get along have more satisfying and more frequent sex, and those who have more frequent sex tend to get along better. "Getting along" and having sex strengthen your relationship because each spouse feels that their partner is most important, and that they are most important to their spouse.

Be aware of your own reasons for having sex—including how frequently you do so—with your spouse, and whether you have sex (or withhold it) to manipulate your spouse into behaviors or decisions your spouse wouldn't otherwise choose. Some couples are fine with encouraging certain behaviors, such as changing one person's mind about a purchase or wanting the other person to mow the lawn. If you are both okay with it, then it's not manipulative. Manipulation is making someone do something against their will.

Past experience, dating, and abuse can all influence a person's views about sexuality. That's why couples will have to determine their own boundaries in this area. Conversations about sex, even between married spouses, can feel uncomfortable. Let's listen in as another fictional married couple, Jennifer and Jason, discuss their concerns.

It's late at night and Jennifer and Jason are snuggling in bed. Jason ups the ante with his hands and words, but Jennifer gets frustrated.

Jason: What's the matter, honey? We hardly ever have sex.

Jennifer: I'm just not in the mood. You can't just make a girl feel automatically in the mood, you know.

Jason: Well, I'm automatically in the mood with you. I wish you'd feel the same way about me. We are married, you know.

What a disaster with a capital D! Both feel less valued. Jennifer doesn't feel like Jason respects her, and Jason feels like Jennifer is less attracted to him. Let's try it again.

Jason: Honey, I love you. I feel like sex is one way of saying that to each other.

Jennifer: That's not fair! If I said that doing dishes is one way of telling me you loved me, would you do them as often as you want sex?

Oh, I feel for this couple! Jason is really, really trying. He wants intimacy with Jennifer and tries to explain what sex means to him and why having it is so important to him. But it came across badly. It sounded something like, "Honey, I love you and if you love me, you better have sex right now." As soon as Jennifer exclaimed it wasn't fair for him to say what he did, he tuned out while she tried to make the point that she was feeling overwhelmed and that this was why she wasn't in the mood. Let's see what it might sound like if they chose to do this differently.

Jason: Honey, thanks for being so close to me tonight. I really can't express in words how important holding you and you wanting me are.

Jennifer: Thanks, Jason. I love you too.

Jason: You probably think I want sex, right?

Jennifer: Um, yeah. You do, right?

Jason: You're so beautiful, I always want to be with you. And when we have sex, it's comforting, especially when I've had a bad day. I also like being intimate with you because I feel like it's the best way to show you that you're the most important person in the world.

Jennifer: So you want to have sex?

Jason: Well, I do, but not if you don't want to. You seem really tired and I want it to be right for you too.

Jennifer: Thanks, Jase. I thought you just always . . . and I felt like you weren't really appreciative of me. I want you to feel that I love you more than anyone else in the world. Do you know what would really help?

Jason: I'd like to hear.

Jennifer: I feel like I'm always cleaning up the house, making meals, and doing laundry. None of those things make me feel sexy, even though I'm incredibly attracted to you, and it takes time and me gearing up for it to be meaningful to me.

Jason (smiles): What if I did the laundry and dishes every night?

Jennifer: How about you do those things for the next couple days, and on Friday I'll be ready?

There are clearly gender differences as to the value of sex and its frequency, and both were willing to negotiate their roles to make the other feel more valued. Jason sidestepped Jennifer's "So you want to have sex then?" by affirming to her that her feelings were just as important as his. And Jennifer validates Jason's approach by calling him a pet name (Jase) and offering specifics about what he could do to help her be more sexual with him.

Similarly, the meaning of sex for each spouse has a lot to do with the conflicts they will have about sex. When there are differences between spouses, such as one person not being in the mood and the other is, or about the frequency with which they have sex, knowing what sex means to each other will help them to resolve the conflict.

CLOTHING

Both men and women are accountable for any conscious deviation of loyalty or interest in their marriage, whether due to their own actions or intent or if they knowingly contribute to it among others. And since immodest clothing can inappropriately attract people outside your marriage, it is important to realize that the clothes you wear each day can make an impact on your marriage.

Let me begin this section by stating my incredible sympathy for women. I know that it is so extremely difficult to find modest clothing, particularly pieces that are affordable and look nice. The culture of today twists God's purpose for attraction by telling women that they have to dress in revealing clothes to look pretty. It can be difficult for a woman who thought she purchased modest clothes, especially with limited funds, to be told that she is being immodest because of those same clothes. We should avoid judging people for how they dress. Men also have an obligation to avoid inappropriately fitting clothing and to be mindful of how they dress.

For both men and women, it's true that some body types have a more difficult time than others with trying to be modest, but the important thing is to recognize that how one dresses sets up a boundary with those who are not their spouse by saying, "This is for my marriage, and only for my marriage."

You have something and someone so much better at home. Be honest with your spouse and yourself about the importance of dress, how it affects you, and your desire to only share intimacy with the one person God intended it for.

You have likely noticed fathers who seem overly strict about what their daughters wear. There is a reason for this. Fathers were boys once. They know of the sexual pressure and biological urges that males encounter, and they know how a girl's "showing skin" or tight clothing impacted their own thoughts. In fact, that sexual pressure is much stronger today than when that father was a boy. Either way, I think a good rule of thumb is to not wear anything you wouldn't want your parents—or Jesus—to see you in.

Another aspect of what you wear is whether you faithfully wear your wedding ring. Some complain that their rings are uncomfortable, unfashionable, or that their rings make them look like they're poor (because they probably were when they got married). I have also heard people say that they simply forget to wear the ring. While forgetting once in a blue moon is human, you should get to the point where you are never comfortable without your wedding ring. Some like to exchange their older, less "bling bling" wedding ring for another ring. If you do this, it is important that you consider how your spouse would feel about it.

Some people are particularly sensitive about whether their spouse's clothes look nice or are in fashion. Wanting your spouse to feel good about himself or herself is admirable, but be careful to examine why you want your spouse to have nice clothes. Is it because you want to be admired? Are you more concerned about other people's perceptions than you are about how your spouse feels? If you feel strongly about the removal of specific articles of clothing from the closet, it is important that you frame your request in a particular way. For example, you might say, "Honey, I know you really love that worn out shirt, and I'm glad you like to wear it. But I really want to get you something newer." Avoid conversations like these:

- Those pants embarrass me and the family.
- That shirt looks horrible—go and get a new one.
- Don't you have any dignity? Get some new clothes.

Remember that while wearing nice clothes often feels good, if you feel that your clothing determines your personal value or that of your spouse, then something is amiss.

Let's take a look at another fictional, married couple, Liz and Jeremy, who are struggling over some differences about one of them not wearing his wedding ring and how each of them dresses.

Liz: You forgot your ring, Jeremy.
Jeremy: I didn't forget it. It's uncomfortable.
Liz: Well, if that's the way you feel about me . . .

That didn't work out well. Liz definitely had the right to bring up the fact that her husband was not wearing his wedding ring. Jeremy made the situation worse by saying he didn't forget it. And Liz took his comments to be a reflection of his feelings for her. Let's try it again.

Liz (as she's kissing him and handing him the ring): Hey, honey, don't forget your ring!
Jeremy: But it's really tight. It hurts my finger when I'm wearing it. Geez, what's the problem anyway? You know I love you and I'm not fooling around. Plus, I don't ever comment about how tight your clothes are on you, do I?

At least we can say this conversation started better than the first. Liz was showing affection while reminding Jeremy that wearing their wedding rings is important. Jeremy initially was responsive by explaining why the ring was uncomfortable, but soon became incredibly defensive about it. He didn't like taking responsibility for what was going on and deflected it back to Liz by saying that the problem was hers—not theirs. Let's see what it could look like if both were more aware of each other's feelings while trying to address a difficult issue.

Liz (as she's kissing him and handing him the ring): Hey, honey, don't forget your ring!

Jeremy: Thanks for the reminder, Liz. You know what? It's really tight. It hurts my finger when I'm wearing it. Can we have it resized or something?

Liz: Definitely. It would mean a lot to me. Wearing the ring reminds me each day that you love me and I love you. And that we are only for each other.

Jeremy (looking even more uncomfortable): Definitely. I feel the same way.

Liz: Jeremy, what's wrong, honey? Please tell me.

Jeremy: It might be hurtful.

Liz: Well, not talking about it is even more hurtful to me. I want you to know that I trust you.

Jeremy: Okay. Um. . . You're really pretty. And sometimes when you wear some of your tighter clothes, I see guys looking at you the wrong way. I guess the way you feel about the rings, well, I feel the same way about clothes.

Liz: Looks like we both need to make some changes, but those changes will cost money. Can we look at what we're willing to give up for a couple months? Because our budget is . . . um . . . tight.

This was an awkward exchange, but it ended up going the right way because they were both willing to consider the other person's needs, and they were both willing to articulate their concerns. Jeremy didn't want to hurt Liz's feelings, and Liz was oriented to making changes—not excuses or accusations.

We'll spend some additional time discussing the boundary of clothing later in the book.

RECOMMENDATIONS FOR PHYSICAL BOUNDARIES

Until you and your spouse determine your own boundaries about affection and proximity, may I offer a few rules or ideas that will strengthen your marriage?

1. When meeting with the opposite sex, limit front-ways hugs to family members and limit side-hugs to friends and co-workers that you and your spouse know and trust. Never touch the leg, squeeze the arm, or caress the arm or back. While eye contact is good, long stares can generate substantial interest. You may choose to extend your boundaries as you strengthen your own marriage or define boundaries in your marriage.

2. Whenever your spouse is present, do your best to ensure that the physical space between you and your spouse is less than the space between you and someone of the opposite sex. Show affection to your spouse with smiles, eye contact, and hand-holding and by leaning into your spouse when your spouse is present and you are talking to someone of the opposite sex. (Remember when you were newlyweds?) When your spouse isn't present, never get closer or show more affection to a person of the opposite sex than you would with your spouse in public.

3. Never use inviting nonverbal communication with someone of the opposite sex. For women this can include twirling their hair when listening to or talking with a man, or putting their hands over his biceps. For men it can mean raising their eyebrows when meeting a woman or teasing her. For either gender, going to great lengths to spend more time with someone of the opposite sex can easily be—or at least be interpreted as—flirting. Winking should be reserved for members of the same sex, family members, and grandparent figures. Practice your expressions in the mirror or with your spouse to see how you can improve.

4. When interacting with the opposite sex, ask yourself what thoughts or feelings you get by being with that person. If those thoughts or feelings would be best if reserved for your marriage, terminate that conversation—and perhaps that whole friendship. Similarly, if you get the impression

the other person's thoughts are improper, trust the Spirit and leave immediately.

5. If you and a member of the opposite sex are having a conversation that tends to limit or isolate your spouse from participating while he or she is with you, end the conversation quickly, find a way to get your spouse involved in a positive way, or hold your spouse's hand, leaning on them and softly gliding your other arm against them.

6. Only offer affection to members of the opposite sex in a way that you and your spouse would feel comfortable with.

7. Always wear your wedding ring. Never let anyone see you without it on and avoid complaining about its appearance or fit. If you want to exchange or upgrade it, talk it over with your spouse first to ensure that you are clear where you investment still is. Value your ring as a symbol of the investment your spouse made in you. If you need to get it refitted for any reason, do it promptly.

8. Tell your spouse if anyone, including yourself, has violated any of the physical boundaries you have set. Your spouse has the right and responsibility to help you maintain that boundary in the future. Explain your feelings about the situation and the other person, and be clear with your spouse that the other person never replaces your spouse's importance and value. Tell them why you feel that way. Ask for their forgiveness and seek to do better. If needed, be up front (polite but firm) with others who have violated that boundary, explaining that certain types of affection are reserved for your spouse.

9. Avoid being critical or judgmental of your spouse while trying to clarify and enforce boundaries. Remember the Atonement is not only for individuals, but also for marriages. Give forgiveness in order to be forgiven yourself.

Please notice that nearly all of the discussion in this chapter has been about members of the opposite sex. Women need female friends to talk to, to relate to, and to get advice from. And believe it or not, men need the same. We'll talk more about friendships with the same sex later in this book (see chapter 6).

Let me state another point—I hope it's an obvious one. It is not wrong to interact with or enjoy the company of the opposite sex. There is no commandment that says thou shalt avoid a man or woman if he or she is not your spouse. But there is a commandment that says to avoid even the appearance of sin (1 Thessalonians 5:22). The key is to determine how much and in what specific ways you want to protect your marriage. Then you need to work with your spouse so that both of you feel loved, respected, appreciated, and admired by your spouse more than anyone else through your shared rules about affection, proximity, and dress.

One last point that needs to be made is that it is not a sin to be beautiful, attractive, or handsome. It's also true that you may not be able to stop all the looks or interest in you or your spouse. But by following certain principles of boundaries, such as how to make, enforce, and repair them, you will strengthen your marriage and your commitment to your marriage. Decide with your spouse where those boundaries are to be and then maintain them.

QUESTIONS TO PONDER AND ACTIVITIES TO CONSIDER

1. What messages did you learn while growing up about interacting with the opposite sex? What did your parents feel was okay to do and what was inappropriate? If your parents were being completely honest, what would they say about how you interact with the opposite sex now? Would you feel that their assertion was valid or skewed? How would they perceive how your spouse interacts with the opposite sex?

2. In what ways do you feel attractive to your spouse?

3. Do you ever feel threatened when your spouse is with someone of the opposite sex? If yes, when and why? If your spouse

knows when you feel most vulnerable (and vice versa), then he or she can be reassuring to you when you would otherwise feel less attractive, respected, or valued. Discuss how this can be done.

4. What are your attitudes about proximity to the opposite sex? At what distance do you feel safe? And at what distance does it feel like you or the other person has crossed the line? Do you have the same expectations about proximity for your spouse as you do for yourself?

5. If you ever feel threatened by your spouse interacting with the opposite sex, provide realistic and fair strategies that you and your spouse can use to remedy those situations.

6. Do you agree with the premise in this book that a woman touching a man or a woman feeling flattered by a man's interest in being in her company can create romantic feelings?

7. Do you feel jealous every time your spouse is interacting with the opposite sex? What realistic and respectful strategies can you and your spouse employ, both in private and in public, to help reduce those feelings of jealousy and potential abuse?

8. Are you comfortable with your spouse having a work lunch with someone of the opposite sex (other than family)? Does it matter who initiates the luncheon? Does it matter how many males and females are there? Does it matter how the meal is paid for? Are there exceptions for how you would feel about those circumstances?

9. In what way is time alone important to you and your marriage? How much time do you typically need in order to "charge your batteries"? What situations or topics do you feel require the most energy?

10. Have you considered adopting the rules listed in this book regarding proximity and affection with the opposite sex (such as the rule about hugs)? What would you change? Do

you see these rules as a promise to each other or something that is more flexible and that can change as needed?

11. How many times per month or week would be ideal for sex?

12. How do you feel when you are wanted sexually by your spouse?

13. Is there something you wish you or your spouse could do like more frequent dates, candlelight, or extra help around the house to increase your desire for sex?

14. What were you taught about sex while growing up, and how have these teachings impacted your romantic feelings toward your spouse? In what ways is sex meaningful to you?

15. How does clothing—its fit or how much it reveals—impact your mood about yourself and others?

NOTES

1. Deborah Tannen, *You Just Don't Understand* (New York: William and Morrow, 1990) 71.

2. Willard F. Harley, *His Needs, Her Needs: Building an Affair-Proof Marriage* (Grand Rapids, MI: Baker Book House, 1996), 12–14.

3. Jerry Jenkins, *Hedges: Loving Your Marriage Enough to Protect It* (Wheaton, IL: Crossway Books, 2005), 16.

4

Verbal and Emotional Boundaries

Have you ever considered reciting or creating a marital promise, and sharing it with your spouse? Here is one example. "I pledge my entire heart to my marriage by being complimentary of you and by protecting my heart and mind from temptation. I pledge to invite God into our marriage to bless and guide us and to grant us forgiveness."

Much like physical proximity, the words that people use relate to affection. What you call your spouse and the tone you speak in signify how you feel about your marriage. The words you say to and about others can reinforce or blur the boundary between your marriage and others. I recall a time when a man said he appreciated a married couple as his and his wife's friends. This was natural and appropriate. But then he started talking about how he likes to tease his friend's wife. It was clear from the person who was talking, as well as the husband whose wife was being teased, that a boundary had been crossed. Unfortunately, in trying to reconcile his misstep, the man said, "I really do love [that man's wife]." Now I know he was trying to reconcile things, and I know he meant it in an innocent, friendly way, but it was still awkward and uncomfortable.

It's imperative that you feel you are the only one in your spouse's life and that he or she knows you feel the same way. A great deal of temptation and hurtful behaviors can be often be averted simply by each spouse filling the "love tank" of their spouse, according to Gary Chapman,[1] author of the *The Five Love Languages*.

I've seen some people joke about "spouse swapping." The first time someone tried to joke with me that they wanted to swap spouses was in 1996. The rare times someone has said it to me, I've told them it wasn't funny—ever. I won't even discuss it. It's out-of-bounds even if its focus isn't on sex. I didn't know that within a few years there would be a popular TV show about wife swapping. I've never watched it or its commercials.

I was nine years old when I first saw "spouse swapping." Two couples in my community decided to exchange spouses. I thought my eyes were playing tricks on me as Mr. and Mrs. Jones (not their real names) divorced and each married a recently divorced Mr. and Mrs. Smith (again, not their real names). Obviously nobody wanted me to say anything to embarrass them. Instead I was told, "They decided it was better for everyone if they married a different person." When I asked my older brother if he remembered this, he said, "Yes, but there was another incidence when this happened, but you were even younger."

I've seen some couples in which one spouse will often romantically tease or offer suggestive comments ("Hey, gorgeous") to an opposite-sex member of another couple. I've also witnessed several couples in which one spouse will give direct compliments to an opposite-sex member of another couple, occasionally saying how cool that person is without saying how cool his or her own spouse is. Even worse, some spouses compare the two out loud. I remember the pain and frustration of a husband whose wife kept telling my brother-in-law how talented he was and how she wished her husband could be more like my brother-in-law.

My point in bringing up these sometimes awkward, sometimes painful situations, is to help couples realize the importance of boundaries. Each of the people I have specifically mentioned in this book were, I believe, trying to do their best, but they did not know what boundaries were needed—or why they were needed. I think we are a little too tentative to speak about boundaries, which has made some boundaries difficult to define. We usually know when things have gone too far, but many people are either too comfortable in their habits or blind to the fact that getting that far is really a process of taking little steps and rationalizing along the way.

One of the ways my wife has increased my feelings of closeness to her or strengthened the verbal and emotional boundaries between us and others, is by sending me little notes of appreciation and love, either through email or on paper. Often we'll call each other when either of us is working "just to say I love you." How couples communicate can affect how close each spouse feels to the other. Consider the tone and content of what you and your spouse discuss—do each of you have an equal voice? Are your conversations filled with gratitude or complaints? When you call your spouse is your purpose to express your love or is it to vent?

Mark Twain said on at least one occasion, "I could live two months on a compliment." Of course, this doesn't mean we should wait two months to give them!

Be willing to revise your expectations of emotional proximity and what it means to you. This set of boundaries can vary greatly, depending on the couple. For example, my grandparents were vocal, both when they were appreciative and when they were upset. Both were opinionated and were not afraid to say what they thought. Phyllis Diller once said, "Don't go to bed angry—stay up and fight." It reminded me of my grandparents. Their marriage was incredibly open, and when there were moments of friendship or tension, both knew they could be forthright, trusting, and validated by the other. Personally, I am somewhat more sensitive of conflict within my marriage than my grandparents were. Neither my grandparents approach nor my own is necessarily right or wrong. The fact is that as a couple you choose your own boundaries, their meaning, and how to enforce them.

Revising and negotiating verbal boundaries is a process, but it makes your marriage stronger.

Consider the following dialogue between this fictional married couple, Aaron and Holly.

Aaron: Honey, why are you so nice with other guys and yet so critical of me?

Holly: What are you even talking about?

Aaron: You're always giving compliments to other guys, but when you're around me, you're critical of me.

Holly: Fine. From now on I'll just shut up.

Aaron started out with a feeble attempt at being nice by using the word "honey," but then he quickly switched to an accusation. Anytime we start with an accusation, the chances for resolving the conflict are quite slim. If someone came up to you and said you were *ever* pathetic, would you *ever* say to that person, "Thank you for sharing your concern. I sincerely appreciate it"? Of course not! None of us likes to be attacked.

Aaron's question puts Holly on the defensive, which is just a way to either be a martyr or throw the criticism back to the accuser. Let's see if there is progress in their second attempt.

Aaron: Honey, I feel that you aren't very nice to me, especially around other guys.

Holly: Really? Are you sure you're not just jealous?

Aaron: Forget it.

Aaron started out with an "I" statement, which shows that he was trying to own his feelings. But then he switched back to an accusation, although not as sharp as the one he used in the previous attempt. Holly either did not believe him or wanted power over her husband. Aaron, sensing no progress was going to be made and a verification of his initial concern (she's *not* nice to him), felt there wasn't any hope of resolving his concern and chose to end the conversation.

Let's try this one more time.

Aaron: Honey, I really need for us to talk about some things.

Holly: Here we go again—another concern and "Let's talk about it."

Aaron: Holly, please listen to me. I love you and want our

marriage to work more than anything else. But neither of us can repair our marriage alone.

Holly: What do you want us to do?

Aaron: Well, for one thing, it seems that you need me to be more outgoing. That's not easy for me. I know I'm shy by nature, but maybe you can help me overcome some of that. You're really talented at networking and meeting people, and I would like to learn from you.

Holly: Thanks, Aaron. That was a great compliment. That means a lot to me. What can I do for you?

Aaron: I think the biggest thing would be if you could help me feel confident in public. When we're in public and I start talking to someone, you often talk louder and take charge of the conversation. I really need your support, not correction, especially in public.

Holly: I feel like I'm rescuing you.

Aaron: I don't need to be rescued—I need respect. I need to know that you respect and admire me more than any other man. That's important to me. Your opinion about me is more influential than even what I think about myself.

Holly: I promise to do better. I know I won't be perfect. But do you promise we'll keep talking about it? I feel this has been really helpful for our marriage.

This third dialogue between Aaron and Holly worked relatively well. There are clear personality differences in their marriage, and even though they probably married each other because they complemented each other, the differences now divide the two spouses. Holly had thought of her husband as a complainer, but once she saw the conflict from his perspective, she had the courage to recognize there was a problem and to seek change. She further validated Aaron and their conversation by encouraging it to happen again.

This exchange, or the problems that led to it, may have also been influenced by gender roles. Women are inclined to want to connect with others. If their husband isn't very good at it, they will often assume that role—feeling judged if their marriage or family is not viewed positively by others. In contrast, some men may limit the conversation between their wives and others, seeking to feel like a leader or of power. Both men and women want respect in relationships, but "respect" is really a tricky word because it means different things to different people—and different things between genders. For women, it is being treated like a human or a real person and being appreciated and valued. For men, their need for respect is defined by how much people look up to (or admire) them. Holly may have felt she was doing her job. She wanted to feel respected when she took over what she felt was her role of connecting with others, but Aaron was offended by Holly interrupting him and knowing that he would lose face or be perceived as a wimp by his male friends.

With regard to mutual respect, there are many different ways you can limit or hurt your relationship with your spouse. These can include:

- Believing that you are better or smarter than your spouse because of your talents, clothing, or job

- Feeling you deserve forgiveness, but being unwilling to forgive your spouse for his or her faults

- Feeling good about your spiritual checklist and pointing out where your spouse is missing on his or hers

- Thinking that you are in charge and that your spouse would be better off just listening to you

- Focusing on yourself when your spouse is down

- Receiving praise from others without acknowledging the help of your spouse

- Criticizing your spouse to make yourself feel better

One couple that my wife and I have a great deal of respect for always "has each other's back." Their personalities are different from each other, yet when they are together, their words always back up what the other person said. There is never competition, shame, or criticism between them.

When you think about the power of words, consider whether you are more like an angel or a devil. An angel's words would heal, help, and give hope. A devil, in contrast, criticizes, tempts, ensnares, and makes others miserable.

Another aspect of emotional proximity and verbal boundaries has to do with how the importance you place on your marriage as compared to another relationship in your life.

For example, how do you view your relationships with members of your family of origin as compared to your relationship with your spouse? Even with your own family members, you should always be clear about your loyalty for your spouse. Let your family know that you will not participate in language discussions that demean or criticize your spouse. Your family will only respect your spouse as much as you respect your spouse.

The same principles hold true when working with youth, whether in civic or religious settings. In fact, this is a particularly powerful and important time to showcase your marriage and its verbal, emotional, and physical boundaries. Youth are extremely sensitive and interested in forming conclusions about relationships, primarily because they are so interested in relationships themselves! When talking with youth, and especially when interacting with youth of the opposite sex, leave them with no doubt as to your loyalty, love, and admiration for your spouse. Do not get so absorbed in your responsibilities or interests for the youth in your life that you find yourself spending more time with them (especially when they are of the opposite sex) than you spend on your marriage. Be particularly careful that you are often with, admiring, and touching your spouse in the presence of the youth you work with. Tell them why you are specifically attracted and completely committed to your spouse. They will learn from your example what a healthy marriage is like.

Be honest with yourself. Acknowledge that youth are especially vulnerable and that they can develop attractions to those who notice them, pay special attention to them, or touch them frequently or in ways that can be perceived as romantic. These attractions are not innocent—regardless of the age differences. More and more romantic relationships are developing among teens and their leaders and teachers. Do not assume they understand where the boundaries are. At their age their sense of boundaries is still under negotiation. And our sexually saturated culture is no help. This is why youth need to know that there are clear boundaries between them and your marriage. Never say or do anything with youth of the opposite sex that your spouse would feel uncomfortable about.

Let me be clear that I have great admiration for youth and especially their leaders. These leaders do an exceptional job. My mother died when I was fourteen years old, and I was the recipient of mothering by proxy from a wonderful woman. I even called her "mom" during my teen years.

But I have also noticed how some individuals cross that line and blur the boundary between their marriage and the youth they work with, typically because they want to be admired or respected by these youth. This boundary blurring occurs when leaders make what they might think are comical comments about wishing a teen were older so he or she could be your boyfriend or girlfriend. It can also happen when a leader alters his or her clothes to appear more attractive or sexy. And it can happen when a leader deliberately seeks out attention from youth of the opposite sex.

Whether with your family, with youth, or in some other setting, the reality is that we sometimes feel drawn to people, roles, or jobs that are not always positive for our marriage. The problem does not usually originate in the people, callings, or jobs themselves, but in how we feel about them. The husband who gains more satisfaction from meeting the demands of others rather than those of his spouse either does not understand how high a priority marriage should have or has not bothered to make his own marriage a high priority in his life. Of course the same holds true for a wife. Ask yourself if answering calls or responding to emails from others is more satisfying than responding to your husband or wife.

As with physical boundaries, how we "position" ourselves verbally and emotionally largely determines how close we feel to our spouse. *Vpmdofrt yjr lrud pm s vp,[iyrt lrunpstf/ Wjrm yjr [pdoyupm pg upit gomhrtd od kidy d;ohjy;u pgg. oy ,slrd s jihr ,rdd/* Translation: "Consider the keys on a computer keyboard. When the position of your fingers is just one key off, it makes a huge mess." Similarly, having your fingers out of position when playing the piano will lead to out-of-tune songs.

How we "position" ourselves verbally and emotionally largely determines how close we feel to our spouse.

How we position ourselves verbally and emotionally is determined primarily by us. In other words, we choose our position. Have you ever seen a couple where both people are incredible, and yet one never seems happy with the other? Or another couple where one of the spouses is annoying to be with and yet the other still exhibits devotion? No matter who you are married to, you can choose to remain verbally and emotionally committed to that person. You make this choice through the boundaries you set and maintain in these areas.

Remember the commandment from God about marriage. "Wherefore they are no more twain, but one flesh. What therefore God hath joined together, let not man put asunder" (Matthew 19:6). Remember, when God referred to not letting anyone divide your marriage, he was also referring to you regarding your own marriage.

Previously, I expressed my fear that many people feel that if they are not having sex with those who are not their spouse or if they are not skipping out in the middle of the night to see a non-spouse, that they are fulfilling their marriage vows. In reality, being faithful to your spouse requires much more than this. True fidelity includes emotional faithfulness, which often manifests itself verbally.

While it is worthwhile to be complimentary to others and to try to build others up, you should consider how your verbal communication is received by others, especially by members of the opposite sex. Does someone of the opposite sex who is not your spouse depend on you to make them feel pretty, respected, or admired? Do members of the opposite sex seem to have a strong interest in talking or being with you? Do you, intentionally or unintentionally, encourage that interest—either verbally or nonverbally? Is that interest acceptable to you and your spouse?

Knowing how you feel, and how your spouse feels, about verbal boundaries is important. Would you be okay telling someone of the opposite sex they look pretty, handsome, or attractive? Would you be okay with your spouse doing the same? Do you know how your spouse would feel? Knowing the answers will keep you and your spouse from having to ask harder questions when conflict over verbal boundaries occurs.

As with physical and proximity boundaries, if you have crossed the line with regard to emotional or verbal boundaries in the past, or have allowed or encouraged others to do so with you, now is the time to take a clear stand. Chances are good that others will continue to cross that line unless you are clear *with them* where your loyalties and expectations are.

People, and men in particular, can be very territorial. If someone crosses the line with you, even if you don't feel like you encouraged their behavior, they will continue to feel that you are interested in them or that you are there to serve their interests and needs. This is perhaps even truer with emotional boundaries than physical ones.

Again, it's important to point out that talking with a member of the opposite sex does not mean that you are bad, wrong, evil, or unfaithful. The question you need to ask yourself is, "What am I thinking or feeling when I am with someone of the opposite sex who is not my spouse?" If those words or feelings ought to be kept within your marriage, then you are allowing someone to weaken your marriage. If you determine what your boundaries are, you can then decide how to maintain them and you will understand how they impact your marriage.

RECOMMENDATIONS FOR VERBAL AND EMOTIONAL BOUNDARIES

1. As mentioned elsewhere in this book, limit direct compliments to members of the opposite sex unless you know that your spouse is comfortable with them.

2. Consider recording how you speak to your spouse throughout the day. The longer you can record, the better because you will forget that you are recording yourself and will not be tempted to adjust how you are speaking. Review your

tone and language, and consider whether you would want your spouse speaking to you in that way. If you cannot record yourself, try to pay special attention to your language and tone with your spouse, and then make adjustments if needed.

3. List all the ways you have expressed verbal affection or affirmation to your spouse in the last three days.

4. Consider how often and how you speak to your brothers, sisters, and parents. If you feel comfortable doing so, ask your family members to tell you how they think you talk about your spouse when you are with them.

5. Set clear boundaries with your spouse about when it is okay to discuss concerns. Be sure to have more positive conversations than conversations that evoke stress or defensiveness.

QUESTIONS TO PONDER AND ACTIVITIES TO CONSIDER

1. What types of affection (emotional, verbal, or physical) do you crave most? Explain why. Give examples of when your spouse offered this kind of affection in the past, why you appreciated it, and how it made you feel closer to your spouse.

2. What does the phrase "direct compliments" mean to you? Are there certain compliments you would like your spouse to give you more often? Do not just say, "I want more compliments." Be specific. Are there any specific words like "wonderful," "awesome," "fantastic," "beautiful," or "handsome" that you feel uncomfortable with when your spouse uses them to compliment others? Why or why not?

3. How do you feel when your spouse is listening to you? Have you shown your appreciation for those times?

4. What verbal or emotional boundaries are important to you and your marriage? How can you each have an equal voice in setting those boundaries?

5. What things do you feel particularly sensitive to or defensive about when your spouse brings them up?

6. Do you agree with the recommendations for verbal and emotional boundaries? If there is anything you disagree with, what do you and your spouse propose adding, deleting, or revising?

NOTES

1. Gary Chapman, *The Five Love Languages: How to Express Heartfelt Commitment to Your Mate* (Chicago: Northfield Publishing, 1995), 23.

5

Social Relationships and Networking

A s newlyweds, we loved visiting with another married couple. They became some of our closest friends. We laughed with them, shared testimony-building moments, and learned so much from their friendship. As much as we valued their friendship, and felt they were like family to us, we valued something else about them even more. They never criticized each other. They never teased each other. They always talked about how wonderful the other person was, whether they were together or apart. It was a rare thing for us to see. And it was wonderful.

Being supported and appreciated and wanting to have fun are instinctive desires in every individual. People typically want to make friendships with interesting people. Finding and making friends whom you can trust, who support your marriage, and who care about you is a worthy goal. But even these friendships require certain boundaries if you want your marriage to be a happy one.

Boundaries are necessary in this area because there is so much potential for joy and for pain. For example, having friends you can relate to, express your frustrations with, and get advice from is actually essential to your health. On the other hand, gossiping about one's marriage, even to the most loyal friends, hurts the marriage. It's ironic that when "other people" spread rumors, they are gossiping, but when we do it ourselves, we think we're just talking. A person who is gossiping often fails to recognize what it really is. The same holds true when discussing your marriage. When talking with a friend of the same gender, if the point is to get advice that is consistent with the gospel, and you know your friend can offer that level of support, then that friend can probably be trusted to give you information you need to strengthen your marriage. I believe it is always wrong to go to a friend who is not your same gender (at least outside of your immediate family) or someone who does not believe in the sanctity of marriage for advice or support for your marriage. Sharing frustrations about a spouse with someone of the opposite gender will likely fuel intimate thoughts in yourself or the other person. Always remember that when seeking help, ask for advice on how to improve the marriage—not just how to "deal with" your spouse. I think any spouse who is seeking help should be honest with his or her spouse about the fact that they are looking for help, but I will admit it may be necessary to make an exceptions if there is a possibility for abuse or if the person fears his or her spouse.

Boundaries are so important in networking, because while there is the potential for great friendships, there is also the potential for harm to your marriage.

Take a moment and consider what boundaries exist between you and your friends. If your friends take more of your time, resources, energy, or affection than you give your spouse, then these relationships have created a barrier between you and your spouse. Time, resources, energy, and affection not only dictate but are symbolic of a boundary between you and your spouse.

When possible, married couples should share the same friends, and preferably the majority of time those friendships should be with others who are married. I have two single (divorced) adult brothers and they agree with me that the dynamics are awkward if they have to spend time alone with a married woman. Of course, this doesn't mean anyone should shun single adults, nor is it implying that single adults are less worthy because they are single. Rather I would encourage you to be close friends with single adults who are your same gender. And regardless of their marital status, you should avoid being alone with your friends of the opposite gender to avoid the temptation that may occur in even the most innocent settings. Even when couples are friends, there is the potential for awkwardness. For instance, most married adults have experienced a time when a husband from one marriage talked mostly with a wife in another marriage, and the two other spouses both felt incredibly awkward. Once again, no matter what the social situation, the important thing is to determine your comfort level (and that of your spouse). Together you can determine what boundaries are most important to you and your marriage.

Recognize that we all have different personalities. This means that sometimes a certain person will seem more interesting to one spouse than another. Even when this is the case, we should avoid pairing off in conversations, as happened above when the husband of one marriage and the wife of a different marriage spent most of their conversation speaking to each other.

ONLINE NETWORKING

Many people, especially those who are younger, report that they feel more comfortable—and find it more rewarding—to hold a conversation online than in person. Social media and online networking have afforded individuals the opportunity to maintain relationships from their childhood, from various locations, and especially with family members who they may not see as often as they'd like.

However, the devil can turn online networking into one of his most deceptive resources for destroying marriages. For some time, the media circulated a statistic[1] that one out of five marriages that end in divorce do so, in part, because of Facebook. While there are several methodological flaws with this statistic, we all recognize that online networking has made unfaithfulness (in any boundary) more accessible. One of my own family members started posting, then chatting on Facebook with a former boyfriend; this interaction moved to talking on the phone, then to secret and late-night phone conversations, and eventually she and her former boyfriend had an affair.

Knowing what boundaries exist and why they exist, serves to protect your marriage, even online.

Whether it is with face-to-face or online networking, you'll want to know where and when boundaries are crossed. Is it okay to befriend those you've dated or had a crush on? I lean on the side of "no," primarily because I believe doing so re-invites the feelings you had for those individuals, especially when you feel disappointed or angry with your spouse.

Online networking can lead to emotional infidelity in more than just cases of online flirting or interest in the opposite sex. For many, online networking takes an incredible amount of time and energy, sometimes to the point that these people avoid interaction with their spouses. Randomly adding "friends" or "followers" can also lead to problems later down the line when you find out through their comments that these "friends" are not interested in gospel standards or your marriage. Evaluate the people in your network or potential network. Consider who and what these people affiliate with and what language they use before adding them to your network. If their language, intent, or pictures are offensive to you or your marriage, delete them from your network immediately.

Much of this emotional compromising occurs when spouses refer to others they are not married to with direct compliments. While compliments are needed, worthwhile, and appreciated, telling a member of the opposite sex that he or she is awesome, wonderful, funny, or more talented than your spouse at (fill in the blank) is likely crossing the line. Comments and compliments should focus on the other person's words, actions, or experiences— "I'm glad you had an awesome time" and "great job!" express the same message without being too personal or implying that you and the other person share anything more than friendship.

SOCIAL RELATIONSHIPS AND NETWORKING

Here is my list for how social networking can impact people and their marriage:

1. Social networking takes time. For most of us, social networking involves understanding how it all works, how to apply it, and getting more "friends" or "followers." We like seeing what other people are doing, and we like to stay connected with people, particularly those we seldom see, through social networking. That time cannot be given back to your marriage.

2. Social networking can be addictive. Have you ever felt that rush from someone "liking" or retweeting your post? Has someone you admired or respected taken an interest in your posts? That emotion is fed by endorphins, which are chemicals that make us feel good. The more we experience that sensation, the more we feel we need it. If you've ever been so engaged in social networking that you find that the day is gone (and you weren't even aware of the time), you may be addicted to social networking. Trying to break your addiction from that high can take a lot of your energy and emotion, two things that are needed for a successful marriage.

3. Social networking lets you be yourself—or somebody else, for that matter. There's something inherently deceptive about the freedom you have to brand yourself online. You can be the person you feel you truly are or the person you want to become. And since everyone wants to be accepted and important, it can be easy to become someone online that you would never want to be in person.

4. Social networking can distort your image of your marriage. If you are active with social networking, you probably have gobs of people telling you how smart, cool, or beautiful you are every few minutes. You may start to wonder why your own spouse isn't giving you that same level of attention or recognition.

Here are just a few boundary recommendations for online networking:

1. The Boundary of Time. Set yourself a time limit with being on social networking sites. When the timer goes off, you're done. Make it a loud timer or alarm.

2. The Boundary of Disclosure. Do not write or say anything on social networking sites that you wouldn't want to tell your spouse about. Just as important, talk to your spouse about your activities on social networking sites and give your spouse full access to your posts, accounts, and passwords. Be clear in your posts about who your spouse is and your commitment to your marriage.

3. The Boundary of Compliments. Do not give anyone of the opposite sex a compliment that your spouse would feel uncomfortable with or that should be reserved for your spouse. I often refer to these kinds of compliments as "direct" compliments.

4. The Boundary of Expectations. Remind yourself that it may be unrealistic for your spouse to give you the frequent level of attention you get online. Question the assumptions about marriages and relationships that you find outside your marriage (including the ones in this book) to determine whether they are right for your marriage.

5. The Boundary of Friends and Followers. If you ever get the impression that someone's interest in you exceeds what you feel is appropriate, even if it is not sexual in nature, be clear about your loyalty and admiration for your spouse. If necessary, delete that person from your networking circle.

I enjoy social networking and am not opposed to it. But I have also seen how dangerous social networking can be. Consider your own boundaries and talk with your spouse about which ones you want to keep, revise, or add to. You'll "like" working together as your marriage becomes more atwitter.

Let's take a look at another fictional, married couple. Karen and Ted have been married nearly seven years, and Ted is reminiscing a lot about his high school years.

Karen: Ted, why are you adding those women as your friends on Facebook?

Ted: Hey, slow down! I'm not doing anything wrong. They were just friends in high school.

Karen: All of them?

Ted: It was a long time ago and we're all just trying to be friends. It's nothing. Really.

Mix jealousy and the words, "It's nothing, really," and you've got a strong dose of mistrust. Karen will drive herself crazy wondering what Ted posts on their walls, what they post on his wall, or if he ever chats with them. She might even log onto his account to find out. This cannot end well. Let's try again.

Karen: It looks like you have a lot of friends. That's really cool.

Ted: There are some I wish I hadn't added as my friends.

Karen: Why's that?

Ted: I've added some ex-girlfriends from my past. I really didn't think much about it then, but now it feels kind of awkward.

Karen: Maybe we can talk about who we feel is appropriate to network with online?

Ted: I think that's a good idea. What do you think?

Karen: I definitely don't want to monitor every person you add or accept as a friend on Facebook, but I admit I feel uncomfortable with you adding old girlfriends.

Ted: You know there's nothing there, right?

Karen: I believe you. But I don't know what their thoughts are. I've heard of too many stories where former flings start on Facebook and then . . . that's it.

Ted: You're the only one for me, dear.

Karen: I know.

Ted: You know what? I'm not really sure how I feel about them being my Facebook friends, but I want to respect you and show you that your thoughts are much more important than any memories I have with other people. I'm going to drop them off my friend list.

Given their availability, popularity, and potential for danger, I consider the misuse of social networking to be as powerfully addictive and destructive as pornography. The rapidness of messages, the desire to be "liked," and the opportunity to connect are wonderful in many instances but can be the tool that pushes a person over the edge in his or her marriage if they are not protected by the right boundaries. You and your spouse will need to decide how you feel about social networking and work together to create your own boundaries. I wonder how many people are paying huge sums of money for mobile networking simply to feel the rush of others being interested in them.

The rapidness of messages and the ability to have your posts "liked" by others can be fun, but without proper boundaries, can cause problems for your marriage.

If one spouse is uncomfortable with the other's online friends, Jason and Kelli Krafsky, authors of *Facebook and Your Marriage*,[2] recommends deleting that person from your networking; better to offend a Facebook friend than hurt your spouse. The Krafsky's book is also a good resource for understand general etiquette and ethics in social networking.

What if Ted had felt more strongly about his online network? Could it still have worked out well? Let's take a second look.

Karen: It looks like you have a lot of friends. That's really cool.

Ted: Thanks, honey. I really enjoy trying to remember my childhood memories. For some reason, I forget my childhood and the fun I had if I don't have others reminding me.

Karen: Your childhood is important to you.

Ted: It is. It just seems like I have so many pressures now . . . not that I'm complaining. I just miss those carefree days.

Karen: Ted, I'm glad you had a great childhood, and I definitely want you to have others around you to remind you of that. I admit

I'm a little uncomfortable with you adding some of your former girl-friends, though.

Ted: There isn't anyone for me but you, honey. Please know that.

Karen: I do. And I don't want you to feel like you have to give up your childhood or memories for me. But in the same respect, I feel threatened when your former girlfriends post on your wall. Maybe we could set up some boundaries that will help you communicate with your friends from your childhood, while still making me feel comfortable with that communication.

Ted: I think that's a good idea. What would you think about . . . ?

Ted and Karen showcased a great example of "give and take" in a marriage. Both were respectful of each other's feelings and sought for ways to make things right.

Below is a list of recommendations for online networking and friendships, but as always, consider how they apply to your marriage by discussing them with your spouse.

1. Create as many good friendships as you can with those who support your marriage. Focus most of your friendship net-working on those who are your same gender, especially with those who will "call you out" if you ever come close to violat-ing your marriage covenants.

2. Never chat with someone of the opposite sex, unless it's your spouse or a family member.

3. Do not accept people into your network unless you are cer-tain of what they stand for. If you find out later their prin-ciples are in direct conflict with your marriage or that they do not respect your spouse, delete them.

4. Friends are incredibly important to your well-being. Try to focus on finding friends in a way that will ensure you and your spouse are comfortable with whatever friend—and their spouse—you visit with. Avoid making friendships you feel will have to be secretive because you you spouse would not approve. Unfortunately, there are instances when

spouses can be controlling and not want their spouse to have any friends. This is a form of abuse. If this describes you or your spouse, please seek help.

5. Never post anything that is critical of your spouse online. You may find that your post will always be "there" and that it will invite feelings and comments from those who do not have your marriage's best interests in mind.

QUESTIONS TO PONDER AND ACTIVITIES TO CONSIDER

1. Do you agree that online chatting should be limited to people of the same sex? Are there other rules with regard to chatting that you feel you should enforce?

2. How do you feel about networking for your career with those of the opposite sex? What specific rules should guide your networking relationships with them? Should you accept financial or business perks, such as a free stay at a condo or airline miles, from a friend or colleague of the opposite sex? When might this be appropriate? Why or why not?

3. How do you feel about the proportion of male and female friends that you and your spouse have online? If this is meaningful, discuss why.

4. Do you feel comfortable with your spouse having friendly conversations with members of the opposite sex over the phone? In what circumstances? Why or why not?

5. How do you and your spouse feel about each person's time on the Internet? Be careful not to be critical or judgmental when you discuss this; rather, focus on why certain boundaries make you and your marriage feel more important. Do not accuse your spouse of trying to make you feel a certain way.

6. Why are networking and social networking important to you? What is most important to you about these relationships?

7. Do you think online networking is potentially as addictive or dangerous as pornography? Why or why not?

8. Do you agree or disagree that you should not use direct compliments when networking? Why or why not? Are there particular words or compliments that you would be okay with if your spouse gave them to someone of the opposite sex?

9. Does either spouse seem to dominate conversations, even when those conversations are with people who are primarily friends of the other spouse? What rules can be set up so that both spouses feel they have their voice and that they are not invisible?

10. How do you feel about you and your spouse reconnecting online with past friends of the opposite sex? What boundaries do you feel would be best? Is there a difference between occasionally looking at their wall or page and actively posting on their wall or page? Explain why you feel the way you do.

11. Be creative about offering verbal and emotional affirmation. Does your spouse prefer written compliments, verbal appreciation for who they are or what they do, or something else? Consider putting together something like a spousal resume that showcases your spouse's talents, abilities, and things you are grateful for. (You may want to consider not calling it a marital resume though!)

NOTES

1. The Facebook study was conducted by Mark Keenanv, managing director of "Divorce-Online." For a critical analysis of the study, see "Divorcing hype from reality in Facebook stats" by Carl Bialik in the WSJ (March 11, 2011).

2. K. Jason Krafsky and Kelli Krafsky, *Facebook and Your Marriage* (Maple Valley, WA: Turn the Tide Resource Group, 2010), 83.

6

The Media

I like watching TV shows and movies with my wife primarily because I enjoy watching her reaction to the shows. Sometimes if she is crying at a sappy moment, I'll lean into her and say, "Honey, it's just a show—it's not real." She'll nod her head and say, "I know," and then keep crying. I regrettably acknowledge that I justify what I watch too often, thinking it won't impact me. But I will often repeat things, especially jokes, that I hear on a show. Sometime people will ask, "What was that?" It seemed like the right thing to say in the show, but I am embarrassed when it does not apply to a particular real-life situation.

With the number of televisions, computers, and now smart phones owned by consumers today, it is easier than ever before for people to watch what they want to watch and listen to what they want to listen to. People often watch TV or surf the Internet because they are bored, curious, stressed, interested in something, or sometimes even addicted to a particular program or site. If you find in your marriage that you *have* to watch a show or check a site, even when you haven't gone on a date for months or even when that particular episode or page becomes clearly inappropriate, then you have misplaced your priorities and boundaries.

We need to be cautious about what we watch, even for "entertainment purposes only." The eyes are the gateway to the brain, and when we watch anything, certain pieces of data and emotions are created and stored inside the brain. The brain is a survivor and likes to hoard any information that has a strong emotion attached to it—whether positive or negative. Then later when the brain senses danger or a lack of information, it will retrieve that information from the media for application.

The eyes are the gateway to the brain, storing messages about the marriage. When our marriage is struggling, it will draw upon those messages, whether positive or negative, to guide us.

The brain is an incredibly powerful and effective organ, one that stores years of micro-second data and emotions from our experiences and observation. Not only is it continually storing information, it is also frequently searching for information for you to access and use. Many times, this is wonderful, but other times it can be frustrating.

When we watch other married couples, either in real life or on television, our brains store data about what married couples do. And when we are in a bind, our minds retrieve that information, which then impacts our thoughts and behaviors in marriage. This is one reason why I discourage shows that mock marriage; even if they may seem funny at times, their premise becomes stored in our brains and can influence what we think marriages should be (or not be) like.

This is why watching sensual movies, shows demonstrating domestic violence, or images that promote individual goals over marriage goals is so dangerous. When we are frustrated with our marriages, our brain will do a "search" for any material they can use, and this often leads to temptations or us saying or doing something "stupid." If you've ever had one of those "What was I thinking?" moments, chances are that your brain really was thinking, but it retrieved the wrong file or source of information to apply.

In general, the media has just one double-edged purpose: to get you to buy a product or buy into a concept. Billions of dollars are spent on advertising alone, and I doubt advertisers would continue to spend that amount of money without results.

Of course we all have free agency and will. But our environment serves as a powerful influence for how we view and treat our marriages. Some of what we see or observe becomes so ingrained that we never even notice it.

I lived all of my childhood years in Washington State, and when we went shopping, the checker would always conclude the checkout by saying, "Have a nice day." The appropriate response to the checker was always, "You too." I didn't realize how ingrained this pattern of speech was until I went grocery shopping for the first time on my church mission in Nashville, Tennessee. When the checkout was complete, the checker said, "Y'all come back." My response without hesitation? "You too."

Sticking with the grocery store examples, you've probably noticed that most checkers will say something like, "How are you doing today?" Have you ever seen anyone who starting spilling their guts, crying, and complaining about life? I've never seen it to that extent, but perhaps you have. The reason we seldom hear this or are shocked when we hear about it is that it goes against the social norms of what is expected or experienced.

Similarly, those who are frequently exposed to harmful images or ideas about marriage will be influenced as to what norms should exist within marriages. Many of you may remember the big lawsuits about secondhand smoke, and the tobacco industry saying it's not harmful or not as harmful as others suggest. We should realize that, whether it is with food or messages about relationships, if it is "consumed," it can impact us in negative ways—even if we don't intend for it to impact us at all.

Being exposed to harmful images or ideas about marriage, regardless of whether they are fiction or not, influence a person's expectations toward marriage.

Recommendations for developing and maintaining boundaries with the media. (Note that the following list and the questions to ponder and activities to consider below discuss television habits specifically. However these same ideas and questions ought to be applied to any kind of media, including books or magazines, music, and the Internet.)

Only watch shows your spouse would feel comfortable watching. This doesn't mean that you cannot have different interests—it just means asking yourself, "Would my spouse feel I'm crossing a boundary or line by watching this particular show?"

If and when you watch shows individually, and there is disagreement as to whether the show ought to be viewed, discuss what the show means to each of you and realize that the freedom to choose to watch the show—or the freedom to avoid watching it—is important to your marriage.

After watching any show, be prepared to discuss the images you've seen and what messages were portrayed about relationships and marriage in particular. Give examples for your answers and be clear as to whether or how these things relate to your marriage specifically.

Have fun watching good shows but recognize that even "clean" shows can have unrealistic messages about marriage and relationships. Discuss messages that appeared clean and fun but wouldn't work in real life for your marriage.

QUESTIONS TO PONDER AND ACTIVITIES TO CONSIDER

1. What shows are important for you to watch? What boundaries, limits, or rules should be in place for watching those shows? Determine what activities or needs take precedence over your show.

2. If the time of a show is the issue or if its scheduling conflicts with other responsibilities or needs, simply record it and watch it later. There are also several online sites where you can watch the shows you want, when you want (for example, Hulu and Netflix). Are you and your spouse comfortable with searching the Internet for videos? What lines or boundaries do you feel ought to be in place when searching for videos?

3. What ratings of movies (like PG or PG-13) or what media content (language, sexuality, violence) are you most sensitive to? Why do you think you have that sensitivity, and how does that sensitivity serve as a boundary of protection for your marriage?

4. Do you and your spouse agree with the idea that you should have a frank discussion about the messages portrayed by the shows you watch? What are the benefits and limitations of following this recommendation? Do you and your spouse have any recommendations of your own for how to deal with the messages you receive from the media?

5. Have you or your spouse ever said or experienced something that you realized later was influenced by what you saw in the media? Discuss the impact that the media can have on you individually and on your marriage, both in a positive and a negative way.

7

Finances and Employment

I am the second youngest of six children and have two older brothers. To conserve money, everything was passed down during my childhood years, and much of what we wore or participated in (band instruments, baseball gloves) had some history with at least one of my older brothers. Speaking of poverty, during a period of time after my mother died, our cupboards and refrigerator were bare, and I was frequently hungry and embarrassed. I recognize those feelings as motivation for being a good provider, but there is one question I always keep in mind when I am trying to provide—is this certain thing for my benefit or for theirs?

If physical boundaries are the easiest to see, financial boundaries—and the arguments that accompany those boundaries—are usually the most common. It is impossible to escape the importance of money and the things it buys—like security, entertainment, food, housing, clothes, and more.

Financial boundaries can protect a marriage by helping a couple save and invest for a future together, allowing them to spend money on dates that enrich the relationship, and by ensuring they have money for gifts to celebrate a birthday or anniversary. Part of the reason why financial boundaries are the most common source of arguments is that money is non-recyclable. Someone who gives a hug to their mother can still give affection to their spouse. But if that same person gave money to a mother or friend, there would be that much less money available for the marriage and each spouse. Matter of fact, one of the most common sayings in a heated argument over money is "It's gone!" Even money spent on a spouse is lost, at least mathematically. But giving affection is always considered in terms of what is gained, not lost, regardless of the amount. Where or how each spouse spends money can reinforce their marital boundary or it can damage it. While agreement and resolution about finances serve to strengthen the marital boundary by protecting them, conflict about finances (and more particularly unresolved conflict) in a marriage will weaken that marriage.

Where or how each spouse spends money can reinforce their marital boundary, or it can damage it.

Focusing more on your money—whether you're spending or saving—than you do on the well-being of your spouse is obviously not a good idea. It can breed frustration, conflict, anger, jealousy, and control issues. Perhaps this is why a recent study by BYU researcher Jason Carroll[1] and his colleagues found that couples with higher materialistic values tend to have the greatest conflict.

It's easy to get caught up with how much we lack financially, and too often we think that if we just had more money, *then* we'd be more grateful. Consider the following comments about money, as well as how the alternative statements are an improvement.

What NOT to say about finances	Alternative Statements
We could never live off my spouse's paycheck.	We could never enjoy what we do today without my spouse's paycheck.
Did you see how much was taken out of your check?	Thank you for working so hard for our marriage and family.

How long until you get a better job?	I respect you for how hard you work.
Your company doesn't pay you jack.	You are worth everything to me. Someday, your company will also realize what you mean to their organization.
Your paycheck isn't even keeping up with inflation.	You being willing to work so hard is worth everything to me.
When do you think you'll get a job? I'm tired of being the only one carrying our family financially.	These look like difficult times. Know that I love you, and I know you'll have my back when I need you.

More and more commonly, women are working outside of the home. Indeed, in many families it really does take two incomes for the family to survive. Some women feel motivated to be employed because of the expectations or influences of their personal circumstances, family background and cultural acceptance. Other women do not want to be employed, and wish to be full-time homemakers. These issues can all bring up tension in a marriage.

When there is tension about the husband's income, it is more likely to be focused on why he isn't working, why he works too much or too little, or why he isn't willing to get a better job.

One of the most pervasive myths about money in marriage is the assumption that you and your spouse will have massive amounts of money to spend someday, probably in the near future, and that this windfall will make your marriage even better. However, some people never reach their windfall and for those that do, it's hardly the end of their money problems. I wish I had a dollar for every couple who has told me, "We were Ramen noodle poor when we got married, but those were the happiest days of our marriage." Why? Because they focused on each other and they didn't have money to argue over.

Of course, money is needed for just about everything, and we cannot discount its importance in determining how we live and the opportunities we have. But having more options isn't always a good thing. Each spouse has their own ideas about what to do with the money, and if one person is right, then the other person loses out. They are both living a myth that they can do it alone, or that their approach is the only right way for their marriage.

Money, and who controls it in the marriage, has significant power. Often, one spouse will have more knowledge or experience with financial matters, and he or she will take the role of making sure the bills are paid and the savings are accrued. But sometimes what starts out as a token of respect or trust for one's spouse because of that talent often develops into deep-seated resentment for the other spouse. That spouse now wants to be part of the decision-making. The opposite can also occur, where one spouse wants the other to be more involved in financial matters—but the other spouse isn't interested or committed to being part of the decision-making.

While we should not take responsibility for our spouse's involvement, we are accountable for whether our spouse feels welcomed in the process—as well as how involved we are individually in financial decisions. Much of the tension over financial problems can be alleviated through appropriate communication.

Let's look at James and Lisa who are struggling with how money is spent.

James: Honey, I'm going to buy a new TV, okay?
Lisa: I'm not sure if we can afford it.
James: I'm sure I make enough to cover a stinkin' TV . . .

This is the type of conversation that a lot of couples have, with one spouse looking for an automatic confirmation for a purchase, the second saying it's not a good choice, and then comes the defensiveness. And the conversation, whether it's about buying a TV or clothes, happens over and over again, with each person somehow thinking the outcome will be different this time. Let's try a new approach for a new outcome.

James: Honey, I really want a new TV. There's a sale on the one I want, but I want to make sure we have enough in our account.

Lisa: That sounds like fun—you definitely deserve it. I really appreciate you being willing to look at the finances before making that decision. I have to admit I get pretty stressed about our finances . . .

James: Don't I make enough for a TV?

Lisa: No, honey. You really don't. But maybe in a few months?

This second scenario started off much better than the first, with James being respectful of the couple's money. Lisa is complimentary of James, but then James feels like Lisa is attacking him over his paycheck power. Lisa drives the nail in the coffin by telling him he doesn't make enough money. Chances are quite high that James feels that his role as a husband, and his own masculinity, are being questioned. Let's see how it can be done the right way.

James: Honey, I really want a new TV. There's a sale on the one I want, but I want to make sure we have enough in our account.

Lisa: That sounds like fun—you definitely deserve it. I really appreciate you being willing to look at the finances before making that decision. I have to admit I get pretty stressed about our finances . . .

James: You definitely have a huge responsibility in taking care of making sure the bills are paid. I really appreciate you for doing that. I don't feel like I'm very good at managing money, and I respect your talent for being able to take care of it.

Lisa: Thanks, James. I definitely needed that compliment. You totally made my day. I also appreciate you working so hard. We definitely couldn't make it without your income.

James: Do you think we can get the TV then?

Lisa: I know you really want it, and I want you to get it for that reason. But I'm looking at the finances and they don't seem to be in order to buy a TV. But I think we could put away $200 a month for a TV until we can get one. We were putting that $200 into saving up for a new computer, but I know it's been a long time since you've gotten something you really wanted.

James: I admit I'm a little frustrated—I thought I was making more money than that. But are you sure we'd be okay without a new computer?

This time it went well because each spouse was respectful and sympathetic toward the other. Both were complimentary and they both wanted each person's voice to be heard and valued.

In some marriages, the role may be reversed where the wife is working or making more money than her husband. In this case the conversation pieces are the same, only reversed. No matter what the money-making situation in your marriage, concerns can be addressed and solutions negotiated in the context of appreciation and respect.

Credit card debt is another concern that many marriages have. The average credit card debt per household is about $15,000.[2] Add this on top of an annual average of $58,742[3] spent for daily living for the average married household that makes $73,000 (before taxes), and you have bought yourself a lot of stress. Couples who are trying to save for their future feel their future slipping away as they try to reign in credit card spending. Let's look at Jane and Robert, who are arguing over credit cards.

Robert: Jane, you seriously need to stop charging on the credit card. We're drowning in debt.

Jane: Look, if you had to deal with the finances and see what I see, you'd have a better understanding of why we use credit cards. We don't have a choice.

Robert: But you charge for clothes all the time . . .

Jane: It's cheaper than therapy.

Both spouses feel like they are the only one who "gets" their financial situation, and that the other is out of touch with reality. But neither is willing to accept responsibility for how things are now, nor do their words indicate any trust or respect. Let's see how it can be done the right way.

Robert: Honey, do you have a few minutes we can talk about something?

Jane: Of course, dear. Is everything okay?

Robert: Jane, I hope you know how much I appreciate you. I know you have a lot of pressure on you to stretch our money to make it work, and I know there's a lot I don't see or know about. But I do appreciate it.

Jane: Thanks, Rob. But this isn't just about giving me a compliment, right?

Robert: I am really stressed about our credit card spending . . .

Jane: You think I charge too much, right?

Robert: I know I've been critical of you in the past, and I really am sorry for that. I'm certain I didn't say things the right way, and I'm going to change how I talk to you about money. Can you help me understand our finances so that we can find ways together of spending less and saving more? I'm sure I need help with that also.

Jane: That would be great! I know I spend too much, but I feel like if we have a plan, we could make this work. What do you think about . . . ?

This approach worked because, again, there was respect and each took responsibility for their own feelings and spending habits. This isn't easy to do, but the response you'll get from your spouse will be dramatically different than when you try to "fix" your spouse's spending habits.

Another financial myth is that your spouse would understand your financial viewpoint if they only loved you more. This is simply not true. There are often gender-based roles, communication differences, and varied expectations that affect our thoughts and reactions to money decisions. Similarly, I believe one of the biggest financial frustrations is that husbands think that their wives do not respect their breadwinning abilities, while wives feel that their husbands do not appreciate their ability to take care of the household or in some cases their income-producing employment.

Men will feel attacked if their "manhood" is questioned. One way this happens is when a wife tells others that her husband can't fix things like other men can or when she publicly corrects or criticizes him at a home improvement store or mechanic shop. This cuts men to the core; it demasculinates them. Wives who feel that this behavior is justified or that they're just being honest should consider the angst they feel when they are working outside the home but do not feel they ought to be doing so. Husbands who are attacked in their role as a good provider or protector will feel incredible despair, a lack of value, and may even feel an opposition to God. Women, what if your husband were to tell another woman she was sexy whenever he noticed you were gaining weight? It really is that intense.

Comments like "We could never make it on just my husband's income" often lead men to question their value. Instead of providing positive motivation, his wife's words will likely cause him to get angry or more isolated. I believe that women are capable of making money and fixing faucets, but a man's sense of identity (and even existence) may be shattered when he hears his wife talking negatively about his abilities, or if he hears his wife complimenting other men for their skills but seldom hears it of himself. Few things will drive him away from you faster than being compared with other men, criticized, or shamed for not being able to "stack up" against other men's qualities. In general, men are hierarchical in nature, and if you compliment another man for his abilities, chances are high that your husband will feel you think less of him. He will think you do not want or love him. Instead, praise him for the talents he has and avoid criticism or sarcasm. Your marriage will thank you for it.

The other side of this equation has to do with women in the workplace. While women are more likely to be employed today than in prior generations, many are still struggling with the question of whether they *should* be working. Men, your wife will typically want your appreciation and recognition, and an ear, for what she has accomplished. Praise her for her efforts, talents, and accomplishments, and your marriage will be better for it. Be ready to give her several compliments and to hear of her experiences at her employment. Realize your job is not to fix her problems, but to provide validation for her feelings. This can be difficult, but very rewarding, to do.

Also consider the impact of split shifts, which can be difficult for marriages. For example, Susan may work 8 a.m.–5 p.m. and her husband Fred works 3–11 p.m. Though this may seem ideal for childcare purposes, and there is nothing in this situation that on its own dictates doom for a marriage, split shifts can negatively impact a marriage because couples see each other less. This means that when they do see each other, they have to spend their time resolving conflicts and talking about the things they have to talk about (such as bills) instead of the things they'd like to talk about.

If working split shifts is the only option or if a wife is not happy with her employment situation, couples have the obligation to assess their individual circumstances to see what can be revisited, managed, sacrificed, or improved upon. What conversations will you have with your spouse if you only see each other for a limited time? Is there any room for negotiation about the wife's or husband's employment status or work schedule? Regardless of which direction you choose, realize that the way in which you manage your conflicts is so much more important than whether or not you have those conflicts to begin with.

The key with employment and money is to not let them be in control of you or your marriage. Yes, you and your spouse will likely make more money as you get older, but your expenses will also continue to grow: diapers, team uniforms, braces, car insurance rates, and college. However, we need to be careful we don't adopt the other extreme or the myth that "We will never get ahead financially." This may feel true, and may even be true at the moment, but the reality is that for most couples, you can improve your financial status within a relatively short amount of time. (Yes, you can. This response is for those currently shaking their heads, saying, "No, we can't. You don't know our circumstances.)

The key with money is to not let it be in control of you or your marriage.

Let's look at some of the most common, flexible expenses and what you can do to improve your marital finances.

- Fuel for the car(s). Gas is a huge family expense. Let's say, between the two of you, you are spending fifty dollars a week on gas. Chances are quite good that you can find a way to limit your travel, which will save you money. If you have more than one car, drive the one with better fuel economy more than the gas guzzler. Limit your trips to the store and plan better.

- Grocery shopping. The key to resolving disputes about how much money is spent on groceries or what groceries are purchased, has to do with meal planning, which should be done by both spouses and both should feel they have equal power in what is right. If possible, it's a good idea to eat food that is on sale that week. You may also consider occasionally dipping into your food storage. It usually has an expiration date, and food storage is designed to be used. You may not be the best coupon clipper, but just by getting the Sunday paper you will likely be able to save a lot of money per week. Remember to buy what you'll use, and not just what's on sale. I often will shop on the days when they have the best sales. Ask your grocery outlet if they will accept competitor's prices and coupons. My family saves over thirty dollars per week just by taking thirty minutes to plan our shopping and coupon clipping.

- Phone bill(s). Most people who use their telephone a lot will have unlimited calling on it. But be careful not to pay for a plan that you do not use up. That's wasted money. Overages also cost a great deal, so each time you're getting close to the end of your phone plan's cycle, make sure you know how many minutes (or texts) you've used. If you've made a mistake, call the company and ask for an exception or "middle ground." Consider whether you truly need the most popular phone or data plan or all the perks that come with cell phones today.

- TV expenses. Cable and satellite TV are costs many people don't even think about. Maybe it's a "necessity," "therapy," or non-negotiable. But at fifty dollars or more per month, you may want to think about watching your favorite shows online. For free. My wife called the cable company one day to disconnect the cable services, and the company *asked* us to keep it for free (because we were using an Internet package and they didn't want to lose us to a rival service).

- Laundry. Hanging up your clothes to dry does not mean you're a "red neck." Find a space where you will not notice them and where they can dry. Not only will it save money in the short term, but it also saves you money in the long term by having your dryer last longer. And you don't have to clean out the lint.

- Eating out. Have you considered taking a cold lunch to work? How about going without your little morning pick-me-up? It does take time and discipline, but it is possible. Start slow if you need to, gradually decreasing how often or how much you spend eating out each week until you meet your goal.

- Be smart with your outsourcing. If there are tasks your kids can do, why not pay them instead of somebody else? I know of several entrepreneurs who hire their kids, thus building their kids' talents and pocketbook, while keeping the money in the family. Our children help with our grocery shopping, fixing computers, mowing the lawn, and babysitting.
- Clothing purchases. Shopping at thrift stores is "in."

On another level, employment can also cause conflict within a marriage and within the hearts of married individuals. I have seen many emotionally and physically compromising situations take place between women and men in the work place. Of course, collegiality and respect for each other are needed, but there's a line that is too often crossed.

Let me share a personal example. I was teaching a class once when one of the students yelled out, "Dr. Cook, I love you!" I admit it took me by surprise. Was it Christlike love? Romantic love? No, it was likely a "You are curving the exam grades, so instead of a B, I'm getting an A" kind of love. The kind that only lasts until the next exam. Thankfully I was given the impression to lift my left hand and slowly wave from left to right, pointing with my right hand to the ring. The class laughed and seemed to appreciate my response to what many felt was a somewhat awkward situation. I hope I made an impression for that student as to what marriage should mean.

At times I also receive thank-you gifts for helping my students and sometimes I happen to see my students in public. Once I went to a bagel shop with my wife and saw one of my students working there. I recognized her because I knew she had serious difficulties with her pregnancies and I had made special and frequent accommodations for her exams and papers. We exchanged pleasantries, and I said I was glad she was able to work again. As I was checking out, she asked to take the register and rang the purchase as an employee purchase, so I received it for free. It was a nice gesture, and I saw it for what it was—a thank-you. (The bagels tasted great too!) But I made sure my wife, Sarah, was okay with it before we ate them.

Although I am in a female-dominated department, I usually do not engage in hugging or touching at work. After several years of being in the same place, all of my colleagues have learned that hugging me is out of bounds, except during rare moments of consolation. Hugging is something I usually reserve for my wife. It is one way I show her that she means more to me than any other woman.

There are a few exceptions, of course. For example, I was quite ill for several months and when I returned back to work, I exchanged hugs with some of my colleagues. If a family member died or if a colleague were leaving, a hug seemed appropriate and helpful.

My hope is that none of you get the idea that I am "high and mighty" or that I frequently experience flirtatious situations. Please know that sharing these experiences is incredibly awkward for me, since I am generally a private person. My point is that they do happen, even with people who have clear boundaries and among those who love their spouses. I wish I had known then what I know now that my boundaries have become such a natural part of my life that they are seldom uncomfortable or unexpected from others. Again, cultural and personal differences will help you and your spouse determine what kinds of physical affection are off-limits.

Another source of potential conflict with regard to marriages and the workplace is in choosing appropriate clothing to wear to work. Everyone wants to look nice when they are dressing for work. Unfortunately, the world's view of nice greatly alters what people wear and how much is exposed. Many women truly do not understand how they impact men with their clothing choices. They dress the way they do because they want to look pretty and they enjoy the attention they get from others. Many other women are aware of the affect they can have, however, and sometimes their actions are even encouraged by their boyfriends or husbands, who see them as their trophy or prize, nothing more than an object that they own.

A recent activity in one of my classes demonstrated that many females understand how much power their bodies have over males but fail to take accountability for it. Let me explain.

I was teaching a course on family stress and coping to a class of about forty-five students. Nearly all of them were female and between the ages of eighteen and twenty-five, and many of them were single or cohabiting. The topic had to do with conflict that can exist between parents and their teen children, and there was a case study about a teen girl who dressed in short and revealing attire. I took a poll and I admit I was surprised that every single person in the class believed that a father has a right—actually a responsibility—to get his daughter to dress in something more modest. I probed and found that nearly all of the students believed that the girl should dress more modestly because of the amount of power her body had on males, especially their thoughts and actions toward her. After the poll I continued with the case study, which stated that the girl became pregnant, and that the young teen father was embarrassed because he felt manipulated into having sex with this girl.

You should have heard the outrage! "All guys 'want it,' " they said. "Just because she dressed that way doesn't mean she had power in that relationship," another voiced. "He's just not manning up," chimed in another. Despite being the teacher, I was the one learning. This was something I had not expected to see, and I hoped to share what I had learned.

It's interesting that this class was completely in unison about the need for the daughter to not wear revealing attire because of how it impacts a male's thoughts and motivations. And yet when the teen male said he felt powerless over the situation, nobody in the class believed it. Matter of fact, approximately three-fourths of the class was laughing, mocking the teen male when they heard of his experience.

As I told the class, it's true that males are often the aggressors in relationships, but we are living a double standard when we acknowledge that females' attire places thoughts into males' minds and then when something happens, we say it's completely the males' fault. Both males and females are often accountable, I think, if they have power over each other and use that power to manipulate or control another person.

I further clarified that I was not referring to rape or sexual assault, which have nothing to do with attire, but rather the power or abuse of another person. I was so intrigued and surprised with the findings from that class that I read the case study in another class I taught, a course on adolescence. Again, the exact same thing happened. In sum, a total of nearly one hundred students and their teacher learned—or relearned—a powerful lesson.

In addition to choosing appropriate attire, men and women need to be careful about how and with whom they spend their time at work. My general policy is to avoid being alone with the opposite sex, whether it is at work or anywhere else, and for the most part I am able to follow that policy. This boundary really originated while I was in graduate school. Another student asked me for a ride to her apartment. I felt awkward about it, but then finally gave in, justifying that it was just a five-minute drive, that she might have had to walk that distance in the dark, and that I was being a gentleman. Nothing happened, but I felt completely wrong inside my heart. I should have at least called and talked to my wife first to ask for her counsel. I have done my best to follow that policy ever since.

Both men and women tend to gain satisfaction and respect in their employment, but it's important that neither feels above their spouse in any way. Egos can get in the way and dictate that one spouse gets more access to the money because he or she is the one who works or works more or makes more. Some spouses like to separate "their" money by opening separate checking accounts or having their own credit cards. The moment one spouse believes they deserve more than the other, a boundary is formed between the spouses instead of between them and outside temptations.

Let's look at another married couple, Sam and Elyse, who are experiencing tension over finances. In this situation, both are employed full-time.

Elyse: Sam, we need to talk about our finances.
Sam: Um, okay. What's up?
Elyse: I feel like I'm not really getting recognized for how much money I'm making.
Sam: Do you mean at work or . . . ?
Elyse: I don't think that you are grateful for my income, even though I make more than you.

Elyse essentially has three strikes against her. The first is that she just drops the bomb on Sam. The second is that she is complaining. And when Sam seeks clarification, Elyse backs him into a corner by automatically assuming he is jealous. This makes her appear critical of his breadwinning abilities. Let's try it again. This time, Elyse has considered her words more carefully.

Elyse: Sam, can we talk for a few minutes about finances?

Sam: Sure. Anything wrong?

Elyse: I don't feel like it's intentional, but I don't really think I'm appreciated for all I do at work.

Sam: Are you saying this is happening at work or . . . ?

Elyse: I feel like you aren't comfortable with the amount of money I'm making. I admit I could be wrong, but it's something I've felt for a long time. Can you let me know if you have any concerns about me working or how much I'm making?

Sam: Well, I really do appreciate your efforts. And I admit I think a lot about breadwinning. I've always been taught that it's my responsibility to provide for the family, and I don't feel like I'm doing a good job if you have to work also.

Elyse: There is a lot of pressure on you to provide. I started wondering why I wasn't more appreciated, and now I feel that I need to be more appreciative of you.

Sam: And there is a lot of pressure on women to be a certain way, but I admit I've been thinking more about the pressure on me. I will do better at showing you more appreciation that's related to your employment. Can you give me some ideas of how you'd feel appreciated for your work?

This interaction went well because both spouses recognized that their marriage was bigger than their own concerns. Both were willing to take accountability for how their behaviors caused stress individually and within the marriage. They were action-oriented, rather than problem-focused.

Let's switch gears for a minute. Consider whom you talk to about your finances. Friends? Neighbors? Brothers or sisters? Parents? Although it's not wrong to solicit or accept advice from others, it can potentially create heartache for a married couple when (1) a spouse feels that the advice of others is more important than what he or she believes is right and (2) when the advice is just plain wrong.

I personally think it's wrong to discuss your financial matters with anyone besides your spouse, unless your spouse agrees with you on whom to trust. This doesn't mean that you shouldn't read any books or do any research on your own, but it does mean that respect, trust, and acceptance are three qualities that are often broken when a spouse values someone else's beliefs about money over his or her marriage relationship. Often the bigger problem isn't the advice received, but the fact that one spouse disclosed financial matters that the other spouse felt were private.

A TV station, KUTV 2News[4] in Utah posted the following on Facebook: "A new study shows about 25 percent of Americans would keep money problems from their spouse. We want to know, what's the biggest purchase you've ever kept from your spouse or significant other?" Some of the participating comments included:

- I'm not part of that 25 percent but my husband is . . .

- Purchase of a digital camera that was 200 dollars. I kept it hidden for a year

- Baby clothes. I'm stashing them up for when we have kids. My husband doesn't know . . .

- That's an easy one . . . My husband bought a 13K Dodge Truck . . . without telling me so I went and bought a Cricut machine.

I removed the names from these comments, but they were not removed in the Facebook postings.

One way to eliminate the problem of secret spending is to develop a "Mad Money" account. Years ago when we were newlyweds, we learned about this tactic from a wonderful speaker at our church who advised the congregation to develop this kind of an account. The account was more symbolic than anything else. It served as an agreement between the spouses about how much money each could spend without the other ever asking why. At that time, my wife and I agreed that a lofty $5 each, per week, would suffice for us.

Since that time, and through various financial experiences, my wife and I have developed a pattern for our private finances. We both know it's okay to spend "small amounts" of money on things we want, without consulting each other. Although we haven't strictly spelled out what that means, both of us are quite frugal in our purchases, especially purchases specifically for fun or for ourselves. If I had to name an amount I would say that anything under $20 per month would be considered reasonable in my marriage. When there are larger amounts involved, we like to call each other for consultation and to see if we agree before we purchase things.

Financial boundaries address so much more than how much money you make and spend. They also have to do with how spouses feel about the house they live in, who can fix fences or leaky faucets, and when they ask for help. Too often couples focus on what is wrong or limiting in their spouse. As mentioned earlier, women and especially men do not respond well when their spouses seem to question their abilities. This means that asking a neighbor for help or telling a neighbor you need help because your spouse can't—or doesn't know how to—do something, is unfair to your spouse.

When I was in college, long before I married, a girl I liked was trying to open the cap on a glass ketchup bottle. When she asked me if I would open it for her, I felt like she respected me, admired me, and yes, *liked* me. She thought I was buff. Then another guy there said, "I'll do it for you," and she passed it off to him. It broke my heart. It was like she broke off our relationship, even though we'd never really had one.

Women, you may think this is just a funny story, but I warn you that men are sensitive to what you say about them and what you think about them.

If a woman frequently solicits help from other men, she should realize that her husband may be experiencing serious doubts about whether or not the woman wants to be married to him. You may think this is crazy. If you still choose to solicit help when you know your husband is uncomfortable with it, watch your husband's eyes to find your answer. This isn't to say that you should have to live in a home with rundown problems; just realize that men whose wives consistently believe in and brag about them will usually go to great lengths to do whatever their wives want done—even if they do not know how to fix or build what the wife needs worked on. Belief in oneself takes time to develop, but if you begin encouraging your husband in little ways, he will find a way to get any job done because he so desperately wants your approval and admiration. Avoid telling your husband something like, "You should contact so-and-so, because *he* knows how to do it." You may not mean it like that or say it in exactly that way, but that is what your husband will hear. In man-speak it translates to, "You little sissy! Don't you know how to do anything? I wish I was with *him*."

If your husband believes that *you believe* he is awesome or can do anything, he will go to great lengths to make you sure you are not wrong. If you do not believe in him, then he will believe the same of himself. Your thoughts about him, or what he *thinks* you think about him, are more important to him than anything in the world.

This unintentional demeaning is not only a woman's "problem." Men who talk about how much their wives spend, where their wives spend money, the fact that their wives' jobs don't pay much, or that their wives forget to pay bills are as much at fault. Men can also make the same mistake of asking a female friend, sister, mother, or ward member to "teach my wife" how to cook better food, spend less money, or keep the house clean. While, in general, women are more accepting of help from others, there are always exceptions. As the husband, you should consider the exception before the rule and show appreciation to your spouse daily for her talents while not focusing on her faults. Believe in your wife because whether you do or not will largely determine her mood and affection toward you. Criticizing or teasing her for her clothes, hair, weight, figure, or makeup, especially in public, is off-limits because she can feel of less worth to herself and to you when you make those comments.

There's another concept that relates to this one. Perhaps it's not a problem in your marriage, but I know I struggle when a male friend or male colleague of my wife offers to pay for her travel, largely because I feel like it's an insult to my ability to provide. I know it may not be intended that way, and I try to demonstrate trust in my wife and be supportive of her and her goals, but it can still be a sore spot.

Teasing is a habit that many of us developed in the dating years, and some spouses use it often to bring up a situation that is sensitive but try to make it funny. Teasing someone about their lack of breadwinning, mechanical skills, cooking, or financial management skills is only funny if the recipient thinks it's funny. It's not "just a joke" if one of you isn't laughing.

If, for any reason, a member of the opposite sex brings up something that needs to be fixed or addressed but that is commonly considered to be your spouse's domain, even if it's only mentioned with the best intentions of helping out, you should either politely but firmly explain that any decisions about that issue are made by your spouse so that person should talk to your spouse and not you or you can explain that you will discuss it first with your spouse before making a decision. If you choose the latter route and you and your spouse agree to accept that person's help, be certain that you give your spouse extra attention, affection, and verbal appreciation to show that spouse he or she is still the most perfect person you know. If you feel that the person offering to help does not respect your spouse or is attempting to get your admiration, run as fast as you can and refuse that person's help—no matter the cost.

Financial and work boundaries are some of the trickiest boundaries to deal with. In your marriage, you may decide to have twice as many boundaries as I do or half of what I have. Either way, be clear with your spouse about what boundaries are needed. It is so much better to ask for your spouse's protection and support in advance than to ask for them after a compromising situation occurs.

RECOMMENDATIONS FOR FINANCIAL BOUNDARIES

1. Consider and discuss what employment means to each spouse—financially, emotionally, and spiritually.

2. How comfortable are you now or how would you feel about your spouse taking time to mentor or team up for a business endeavor with someone of the opposite sex? Would it depend on certain factors or circumstances? Give examples.

3. Determine the precise amount of money each spouse can

spend without having to address where it goes. Make sure the amount is equal between spouses. Do not include groceries, home bills, tithing, or any other absolutely necessary item in that decision.

4. Unless your spouse is okay with it, refrain from asking or accepting an offer from a member of the opposite sex to fix or resolve something that is typically the other spouse's responsibility. Show your belief in your spouse by telling him or her, "I know you can do this, but either way I'm still your best friend and only lover."

5. In each of your financial decisions, ask yourself, "Is this purchase or choice something that would build or weaken my marriage?"

6. Never criticize your spouse—and this rule "goes double" in public, regardless of whether it has to do with financial matters or not.

QUESTIONS TO PONDER AND ACTIVITIES TO CONSIDER

1. Are you or your spouse ever jealous or hurt when the other asks a member of the opposite sex for help? When? Why or why not?

2. Do you agree with the assumption that men and women will go to great lengths (regardless of their talents) to please their spouse, as long as their spouse believes in them? Why or why not?

3. How do your childhood experiences influence how you feel about a father and mother working? Give examples.

4. If you had a million dollars in your wallet or purse, how would you feel about it? How would you feel about yourself? Does how much money you or your spouse makes influence how you perceive yourselves individually or as a couple?

5. When is it okay to ask someone (other than your spouse) for

financial advice? What details about your family finances are okay to share? What things are not okay to discuss? Does it depend on who you share that information with? Give examples.

6. Are you okay with other people giving your spouse money? Why or why not? Give examples.

7. Do you agree with the recommendations listed above about finances? What would you change?

8. Do you think that writing down your expectations about how to save or spend money *as a couple* is worthwhile?

NOTES

1. Jason S. Carroll, Lukas R. Dean, Lindsey L. Call, and Dean M. Busby, "Materialism and Marriage: Couple Profiles of Congruent and Incongruent Spouses," *Journal of Couple & Relationship Therapy*, 10:4 (2011): 287–308.

2. http://www.creditcards.com/credit-card-news/credit-card-industry-facts-personal-debt-statistics-1276.php

3. Average income for married couple in 2008 was $72,743. http://www.census.gov/compendia/statab/2011/tables/11s0699.pdf.
Total expenditures for family of 72,743: http://www.census.gov/compendia/statab/2011/tables/11s0687.pdf

4. KUTV 2News, http://www.facebook.com/KUTV2News, October 11, 2011.

8

Being Parents and Boundaries with Children

"**M**y mom is always posting things about me on my Facebook wall. She'll post baby pictures—pictures of me in the bathtub—and then she'll tag me. She posted old prom pictures of me with a previous boyfriend, then tagged me and him. Then she found out I had a new boyfriend recently and asked him to be her friend on Facebook." This quote was shared by a young adult student who volunteered this information.

Parenting is of great importance since we know that those who neglect, abuse, or offer poor examples to their children are accountable. Although the parent-child relationship is important, the scriptures are clear about the fact that we are to cleave unto our spouses and none else. Healthy families prioritize their experiences by making sure that married couples are first loyal to each other in the ways we have already addressed. Unfortunately, parents can sometimes use their children as emotional confidants when they really should be confiding or trusting in their spouse.

Particularly having a baby for the first time can be challenging for a lot of couples. In my own research, I found that approximately one-third of all couples experience a decline in their marital satisfaction between the pregnancy and the second birthday of their first child. There are many reasons why this would be the case: lack of sleep, more stress, financial worries, and the list goes on and on.

But the list reflects a division between couples that occurs during a period of time when they need to be most strong. Men who go with their wives to the doctor often report being "invisible" to the medical professionals; they are not the patient nor the "parent." While it's true that natural childbirth programs, such as Lamaze, are designed to bring the father back into the picture, my observation, research, and experience all suggest that most men are pushed out of the way. Husbands now shift their attention to what others tell them is their most important job, to make money, while wives start to feel that they must be the experts and will be judged by how their child acts, looks, and speaks.

New parenting couples start to have their boundaries blurred and begin to accept (or despise) that this is just how it's done. It is very important for couples to recognize the changes in their marital boundaries, and those who start with strong and clear boundaries often have strong marriages as parents. One of the best books on helping couples recognize how changes in parenthood impact their marriage is a book by Carolyn and Philip Cowan, *When Partners Become Parents*.[1] It discusses the role changes, such as how parenthood changes a person's thoughts and experiences, and how to limit the contention that can occur when boundaries become blurred.

For new fathers struggling to balance work with family, I also recommend *Working Fathers: New Strategies for Balancing Work and Family* by James Levine.[2] Levine talks about how there has been a great deal of cultural change and acceptance for mothers who have professional occupations, but that policies designed to help the "working parent" often misses helping the working father.

My scholarship has also focused on distracted driving. I believe that this can definitely work as an analogy to marriage boundaries. Let's say you are driving down the road and you need to reach into the backseat to offer juice or cookies to your kids or resolve an instance of sibling rivalry. All of those things are important, but reducing your attention on where you are and where you're heading greatly increases your chance for an accident. Similarly, we need to meet the needs of our children, but we also need to draw the line in favor of our marriages in order to know where we are in our relationships and how to get where we want to be as a couple.

Are you focused on your marriage, or are you allowing other things or people to distract you from the destination you want with your marriage?

Of course, we should trust our children, and we would hope they would trust us. But your loyalty must be, above all else, to your spouse. This means that if your child starts saying negative things about or to your spouse, you need to step in and make it clear that they are out of line.

Years ago, my wife and I decided that, despite some differences in parenting ideology, we would support whoever had made the first decision. A simple example of this is when our children will ask my wife if they can have a cookie or watch television. If she says "no," then I am committed to her decision, even if I have a difference of opinion.

Another way of creating healthy boundaries between your marriage and your children is by being sure that you are not critical of your spouse when your children are around. As we have discussed, others will treat your spouse how you treat him or her.

Many married couples reason that they will spend more time together "when the kids get older," "when we make more money," or "when we can." Couples should be mindful that marriage is never static and that they will not likely jump from Point A to Point E without going through B, C, and D first. Postponing working on your marriage now will impact your marriage later. There is no "cutting" in the marriage line. If you want to have a happy marriage in the future, you've got to focus on having a happy one now. It takes time.

Another way of creating healthy boundaries between your marriage and your children is by treating your spouse "right" around your children.

There are differences of opinion as to whether parents should argue in front of their children. It can be healthy for children to see their parents resolve challenges, not only because it teaches them how to do it themselves, but also because they develop trust in their parents and in their parents' marriage. Unfortunately, too often children see only the arguments and not the resolution. Either way, if the tone or content gets personal, you should discuss things in private, and both spouses should apologize to the children because they were not treating their other parent right.

Telling your children stories about your courtship is both exciting and humanizing. Children love to know their parents were "real people" at one time and enjoy hearing about how the two of you met. Tell them what you appreciated most about your spouse, and then explain how those qualities have improved over time. Children will know that you love them when you are sure to show your love for your spouse. Parents are a part of their child, and if their parents are "broken," the child will also feel that way. Your love story with your spouse serves as the beginning of your child's identity, and children like to know the whole story, including the juicy stuff—even if the younger ones scream, "Ooo-oooo."

Telling your children stories about your courtship is both exciting and humanizing.

Going on dates, reading, or watching a fun show together as a couple is important to rekindle the feelings you had while you were dating. It breaks the monotony and reduces the pressure of trying to be a good parent all the time.

Some married parents have their children unintentionally serve as boundaries between them and others they may not know or trust. Some specific examples include allowing your children to be an excuse to change the dynamics of a situation or to leave that situation entirely, whether it is with someone of the same gender or the opposite one. Did you ever ask your child to tell you they needed something when you were with someone who annoyed you? Have you ever gotten off the phone by telling the person on the line that your child needed you when they didn't really? Have you ever encouraged your child to interact with someone you otherwise would not trust to be alone with you?

If a repairman is at her house, a mother—and the repairman—may feel more comfortable when there are children around. Clearly some of the gravest dangers in marriages are when one spouse is alone with a member of the opposite sex. Having children around can increase the boundary between a spouse and another person. You would not want to do anything inappropriate, and there is power in having another person there to tell others if anything inappropriate happens.

There is a difference, however, between allowing children to serve as natural boundaries between you and others, and *expecting them* to serve as those boundaries. Some parents go into places or situations they know are inappropriate but feel more comfortable doing so because they have their children with them. It is a heavy burden for a child to be expected to protect a parent from unwanted advances, inappropriate interactions, and false accusations.

Most children do not know that their parent want them to play that role. I definitely do not recommend telling young children any specifics about how they are boundaries between you and others. If they are older, you can simply say something like, "I feel more comfortable when you are with me." Teens and young adults are likely more aware of the situations, nuances, and interactions in which they become barriers and may be more willing to give active help in difficult situations.

RECOMMENDATIONS FOR HEALTHY BOUNDARIES BETWEEN PARENTS AND CHILDREN

1. Never talk negatively about your spouse, especially in front of your children.

2. Compliment your spouse, especially in front of your children, explaining why you are blessed to have that person as your spouse.

3. Tell your children positive stories about your courtship.

4. Never tell your child something you wouldn't tell your spouse.

5. Never "jockey" for position or approval from your children by making your spouse look less favorable.

6. Go on dates or at least specify times when the two of you will only discuss the things you like about the other and have fun as a couple. Consider making a commitment to not discuss the children during these times.

QUESTIONS TO PONDER AND ACTIVITIES TO CONSIDER

1. What are your thoughts about what to do when the two of you differ on how to raise children? How can you avoid having children play on those differences?

2. What time and activities do the two of you have planned for the next couple of weeks? How can you make them more fun and creative? Do you both agree that you shouldn't discuss your children during these times? Why or why not?

3. Keep a journal for how many times you compliment your spouse in front of your children. This is not a competition, so avoid setting it up that way. Document how your compliments over a period of a few weeks impacts how your children feel about your spouse.

4. During family activities or outings or at bedtime, tell your children fun and uplifting stories about your courtship with your spouse before you got married.

NOTES

1. Carolyn P. Cowan and Philip A. Cowan, *When Partners Become Parents* (New York: BasicBooks, 1992).

2. James A. Levine, *Working Fathers: New Strategies for Balancing Work and Family* (Boston: Addison-Wesley Publishing Company, 1997).

9

Some Boundaries for Each Stage of Marriage

The previous chapter discussed boundaries with regard to children. But these boundaries can vary greatly depending on the age of your children and the stage of your marriage. In this chapter, you will find a brief discussion of several different stages of marriage and what kinds of boundaries ought to accompany them. Since the format of this chapter is slightly different, there are no accompanying recommendations and activities; however, I encourage you to discuss the questions in this chapter and consider how the concepts covered relate to your personal circumstances. No matter what stage you and your spouse are currently in, you will find that boundaries can enhance your relationship now and provide a clear path for your future together.

ENGAGED/GETTING MARRIED
Boundary Theme: Expectations

Deciding to get married is an exciting and perhaps stressful decision. Love is powerful, but it will not solve all the challenges you and your spouse will have. Now is an important time to be clear about what your marriage means to you and what you expect it to be. Be clear about your individual role in the marriage. Try to understand how past experiences, your family of origin, and your friends can impact your view of marriage—in good ways and bad. Recognize that your spouse is perfect for you, but not truly perfect. You should also understand that you (and not your spouse) are responsible for how you feel—now and in the future.

What expectations do each of you have for the future? Where do you want to live? How do you feel about mothers working outside of the home? Are you each going to maintain friendships with the opposite sex? What boundaries need to be created between your marriage and others at this time?

Remember that having differences is not necessarily a problem. The important thing is to be able to create or negotiate boundaries as a couple.

FIRST-TIME PARENTHOOD
Boundary Themes: Time, Energy, and Resources

Many couples decide that they want to have children, yet few couples discuss specifics about raising children. Who is going to do what? Is it okay to ask for help? Who should you ask for help? Will you take turns feeding the baby or changing diapers? Are both parents going to work?

Time and energy will be reduced when your children come along, so it's important that you are as effective in your boundary management as possible. Are you able to see things from your spouse's perspective? When you negotiate roles, responsibilities, and boundaries, do you still affirm your spouse's value?

One of the most common arguments among first-time parents is about what the father ought to do. Realize that today's mothers and fathers have different expectations than many of their parents, so patience and an understanding that parenthood is a process are keys to success.

Discuss with each other how your childhood experiences influence your idea of what a good parent is. This is a time of sacrifice, and investment but the better you are at understanding and working within boundaries as a couple, the better off you will be. Remember that having a child is one of the greatest experiences a person—and marriage—can enjoy.

Remember to give your marriage time, even if it's minutes at a time. During that time, only talk about each other, and not your child. Give compliments and appreciation to each other and, if possible, go on dates. The transition to parenthood often leads to more traditional attitudes and divergent behaviors between spouses. Men tend to worry more about providing income, and women tend to spend more time and attention focused on how to raise a child. While working in your specific roles may be the most efficient method at the time, creatively spend time together that emphasizes your similarities, shared dreams, and goals for lifting each other.

Having a baby is generally expensive, and for most families being parents takes up a large share of their financial resources. You may need to find some creative, inexpensive, and maybe even short dates. With your time, energy, and resources in such scarce supply, now is a good time to leave phone messages, poems, and love notes throughout the house. When you do have time together, cherish it and each other.

PARENTS OF A YOUNG CHILD (AGE 2–11)
Boundary Theme: Growing Up

The early years of your child's life are good predictors for how each of you will parent, but keep in mind that you are still learning and developing in your roles as parents for years to come. For example, sometimes fathers become much more involved with their children as their children become more autonomous and able to move. One thing's for sure, this is a fun time to watch your child grow, change, and learn.

Even if you and your spouse have already discussed discipline, it's a good idea to talk about it again. Having consistent rules and expectations, through the process of negotiation, is vital not only for your child's development, but also for your marriage. You should also have a plan for how to respond when the two of you disagree on discipline. Each of you should try to maintain a positive role in your child's life but ensure that your spouse also has that same opportunity.

As your child becomes more independent his or her needs will change but they will never disappear altogether. Your young child can talk, yell, hug, sleep longer, and hit. Be clear about affirming both the value of your spouse and your respect for him or her. Realize that your child is learning from you about how to treat your spouse.

PARENTS OF A TEENAGER
Boundary Themes: Power and Role Models

Teens often try to obtain more power than they have previously had over their parents. Chances are that they are getting smarter. This means they will test your boundaries. If mom says something they don't like, they'll go to dad. Enforce the rules given by whichever parent they go to first.

As mentioned previously in the book, teens are perceptive of relationships. They may think that mom and dad are "sick" or "epic" when they kiss, but the reality is that they desperately need to see examples of couples who truly love each other. Sexual and exaggerated body images haunt many of these teens' minds; knowing that each parent is loved for who they are—and that the same holds true for their children—will work wonders on your teen's self-esteem. It will also give them the confidence and desire to seek out and eventually marry someone who treats them the way their parents treated each other.

PARENTS OF A YOUNG ADULT
Boundary Theme: Letting Go

Young adulthood has changed drastically within the last generation. More and more young adults are living at home longer, taking a longer time starting their careers, and staying in school longer. This can be frustrating for parents who always thought that becoming a legal adult meant it was time to be a fully functioning adult.

It isn't uncommon for some parents to have difficulty letting go of their little girl or boy. While this is understandable, it can also signal the reality that their feelings are somewhat displaced if they have focused more on their children than on their own marriage.

Whether your young—or even "old"—adult child is still living with you or not, consider carefully where you place your time, energy, and priorities. Your children will look back and thank you for setting a good example.

10

Boundaries of Roles and Responsibilities

My children usually like to go shopping with me—their dad. It may have something to do with me letting them get a treat when they help me shop. Once, as we were checking out, a female checker kept scowling at me while my kids were acting out. There wasn't any conversation between us. No "How was your day?" or "Did you find everything you need?" At the end of the checkout, I started to walk away, and she said, "Now you know how we feel."

When we get married, most of us feel that love will conquer all. But as we experience life together, we learn that love will not do the dishes, gas up the car, or change a dirty diaper. It may encourage us to do those things, but it will not do it by itself.

Our society is definitely changing at a rapid pace. Did you know that fathers were not allowed in hospital delivery rooms until 1970? Now men are expected to be in the delivery room, attend Lamaze classes, and burp babies. Being expected to be one way and knowing how to do it are two different things. Many fathers today did not learn from their own fathers what is expected of them now. Or for younger fathers, their own dads may have been the first to learn how to do these things, and it may be difficult for them to know what they should do.

If you've been married for some time, you've probably already gotten into a groove as to who does the dishes, who does the laundry, who pays the bills, and who grocery shops. But how did you come to those decisions? Did you discuss it or were certain things just dumped into one spouse's lap?

It may seem a little awkward, but my philosophy is four-fold: (1) If it bothers me, I do it. (2) If I have time, do it. (3) If I don't like how others do it, I do it. (4) If I can provide service to you, I'll do it.

But what works for me won't necessarily work for you or your spouse, especially if one spouse is more particular about cleanliness than the other. That's because everyone has different expectations about household roles and duties. For example, I have a different standard of what is "clean" than my wife does. Over time, I have found what I do well—and what I don't—and we negotiate what happens. "Honey, I'm going to do my best cleaning the kitchen, but I know you like it a certain way. I'll do what I can, but I want to know you appreciate it even if it doesn't meet your standards." Sometimes she'll prefer to do that chore herself and other times she accepts that my eye for details in cleaning is not as good as hers. Sometimes we will work together on chores. For example, sometimes I will scrub the dishes, then hand them off to Sarah who puts them into the dishwasher because she likes to load them a certain way.

Telling your spouse that you do more dishes or laundry, make more money, or spend more time with the children than other people do means that you are basing your worth off what your spouse or the average person does. Some scholars refer to this as "social comparison." Often this can creep into a marriage when one spouse is upset with the other. For example, have you ever responded to your spouse's frustration with you by saying or implying that you are better than others (particularly of your same gender) in what you bring to your marriage? Our environments set the standard for what is acceptable, and if we surpass that standard, we assume we are doing what's needed for our marriage.

Men, do not discount your power and responsibility to help with as much housework as you can or even to take the primary responsibility for household chores as needed. Laura Brotherson, in her book *And They Were Not Ashamed: Strengthening Marriage through Sexual Fulfillment*[1] tells a funny story about a married couple who struggled with their sex life. The husband was particularly dissatisfied and did everything he knew to get his wife in the mood, including buying her flowers. Someone told the husband that his wife might simply be too tired for intimacy and that if he helped clean the house, it might restore her energy and interest.

Brotherson goes on to describe the housecleaning that the husband did in earnest while his wife was away. When she got home, she told him she would meet him in the bedroom. The man, clearly exhausted after his long day of cleaning, said he was just too tired. The point isn't to get overworked, but rather to recognize that sharing the load will help you and your marriage—and not just sexually.

I actually prefer doing my own laundry at times. It's not that I'm all that good at it, but I don't like it when my clothes stay in the dryer or with other clothes, and I dislike having to iron my shirts. Part of my preference likely has to do with my childhood or the fact that my mom died when I was young and I had to start doing my own laundry in my teen years. We all make compromises, but it's important that each spouse feels appreciated and respected and that there is a balance to who does what.

Don't get completely set on drawing lines in the sand as to what each person has to do. The roles need to be flexible according to the family's needs. You should also pay attention to how you feel the Spirit is directing you. And there are times when you can change your roles to show your spouse your love.

Sometimes gatekeeping occurs. This happens when one spouse feels territorial about certain roles. Then when the other spouse tries to help out in that role, the spouse who thought they were helping ends up getting criticized. As you set your boundaries, you may want to consider whether certain tasks should be set in stone or if you ever want to rotate them. If you do decide to rotate, you may just gain a new appreciation for each other!

In the early part of my marriage, the most common foods we had were homemade spaghetti (with regular tomato sauce) and homemade breadsticks. When we felt really wild, we'd add a little bit of oregano to the sauce and cheese to the breadsticks. While it's true that we were hungry for other things that would cost us more, I look back and envision each noodle and breadstick scrawled with the letters, "I l-o-v-e y-o-u." That's what my wife's meals meant to me.

More recently I have found that I enjoy cooking, and even better, we have a daughter who loves to cook. When I make something unexpected or really yummy, my wife will post her appreciation for it on Facebook.

In the early years of our marriage, I realized my wife had serious troubles with managing money. It wasn't that she spent a lot of money, but rather she just difficulties keeping track of what was spent or what it was spent on, leading to multiple experiences with bounced checks. Over time, my wife developed a much better talent for organizing finances than I had, and now she has been our financial organizer and planner for years. Plus, I was never good at keeping track of how much we had in our account either, so while I never bounced a check, our uncertainty about exactly how much we had in our account made us always question ourselves when considering a purchase.

Let's take a look at another fictional, married couple who is having some difficulties roles and responsibilities. Neal is employed full time and has just returned home, and Eva is a full-time homemaker.

> Neal: Hi, honey. Oh, wow. This place is crazy.
> Eva: I've been real busy.
> Neal (laughs): I can see that.

Neal needs an attitude adjustment. He enters the house and it's messy, but his focus is more on the mess than on his wife. Let's see what their second attempt looks like.

> Neal: Hi, honey. How was your day?
> Eva: Pretty wild, as you can tell.
> Neal: Yeah, it looks crazy in here.

Round two started a little better, with Neal inquiring about Eva. Once she said it was "wild," he should have made sure what she meant before responding with, "Yeah, it looks crazy in here." Neal may have been trying to make a tense moment into something more humorous, but if Eva doesn't laugh, then they're both left feeling that the other person doesn't understand them. Let's try it once more.

Neal: Hi, honey. How was your day?

Eva: Pretty wild, as you can tell.

Neal: Are you okay?

Eva: I guess so. I just feel so discouraged having to do the same thing over and over again. I want to be a full-time homemaker, but I feel like I need a hobby or something.

Neal: Sounds like you need a break from the routine.

Eva: Definitely.

Neal: Hey, I have an idea. I'll take the kids all evening while you think of something you'd like to do. Then we can look at our finances and schedules to make sure you get the break you want and need.

Neal did a better job with focusing his attention on Eva. He still saw the mess, but it wasn't as important as his wife and her feelings. He restated what he thought Eva was saying, seeking clarification, and then offered more help so that she could get what she needed.

Whether because of past experience, current necessity, or religious beliefs, many times spouses will assume that the other person knows exactly what he or she is supposed to do. And if their spouse doesn't do those things or perform that role a certain way, there can be conflict.

Focusing on your spouse and communicating in a way that shows respect are keys to negotiating the roles and responsibilities in your marriage.

RECOMMENDATIONS FOR ROLES AND RESPONSIBILITIES

1. Keep track of everything your spouse does for you and the family. The moment you lose track is the moment you lose gratitude for what your spouse does. Do not compare what your spouse does with what you think you do.

2. Don't become territorial. If your spouse helps you out, show your appreciation. If you can see that your spouse is becoming overwhelmed, get involved and help out. Be clear that you want to help, but be sensitive to what your spouse says as to what he or she really needs or if he or she wants to continue to do it alone.

QUESTIONS TO PONDER AND ACTIVITIES TO CONSIDER

1. "Who did what" in the family you grew up in? What about in your spouse's family? How does your history influence how you think things ought to be in your marriage?

2. What roles are exclusively the husband's and which are the wife's? Are you willing to make accommodations when needed or requested?

3. How do you feel when your spouse offers to help? Does it depend on what is being offered? Give examples.

NOTES

1. Laura Brotherson, *And They Were Not Ashamed: Strengthening Marriage Through Sexual Fulfillment* (Seattle: Inspire Book, 2004) 49–50.

11
Spiritual Boundaries

While the spiritual checklists (did I say my prayers, read my scriptures, and so on?) can be helpful to make sure you are on track, we must realize the Savior offered Himself because He knew we would not be perfect in this lifetime—or that we could only become perfect with His Atonement. Be careful not to judge yourself or your spouse too harshly if you or your spouse does not fit the ideal image you have for a parent or spouse. Perfection was never a requirement for receiving God's blessings.

The longer you have been married, the more likely it is that you have been hurt at one time or other by your spouse. Or that you have hurt your spouse. Personality, past experiences, and perception of your spouse's intent will influence your ability to forgive.

Many people use the Atonement daily to invoke its healing power, usually by asking for forgiveness of their own sins. I suggest that most people are less likely to ask for that power to help them forgive others. Why would this be the case?

For some, they do not feel like they are being treated fairly. They refuse to forgive their spouse until their spouse changes their behavior. Often they feel offended. They reason that, "If my spouse loved me, really loved, me, then my spouse would change and then I would be able to forgive." This approach rarely helps a person feel better about a marriage or facilitate any change. Even if the offending spouse did change, the offended spouse would likely feel that the offender was only doing it to stop the nagging.

Harping on your spouse or nagging your spouse to change usually increases the boundaries between the two of you, increases conflict, and makes both of you feel less respected or loved. No matter how hard the offender tries, the offended spouse ends up thinking, "There, you see that? I tried to tell him what he needed to change for me to be happier with him, and he didn't get it. He wasn't willing to change for me."

Let's look at another fictional married couple, George and Debbie, who are arguing over spirituality.

Debbie: George, I really wish you would be a better leader in our family.
George: That's because you're not a good follower.

Okay, definitely not the best approach. Let's try it again.

Debbie: George, thank you for everything you do.
George: Um, okay. You're welcome, I guess.
Debbie: Now, what I really wanted us to talk about is that I wish you were a better leader in our family.

Crash and burn! Debbie only brought up a vague compliment in order to manipulate George into what she wanted him to be. Let's try it one more time.

Debbie: Thanks, George, for leading us in prayer last night. It means a lot to me when you do that.
George: You're welcome. I know I don't say it very often.
Debbie: Well, it means a lot to me. I see you as such a great leader of our family, and you initiating a prayer helps me feel closer to you.
George: I guess I struggle with leading prayers because I don't feel very respected.

Debbie: I'm sad to hear that. I definitely respect you, but I admit I may not always show it as well as I should. Do you have any examples of how I could help you feel more respected?

George: I don't know.

Debbie: It's okay if you don't have any specifics. I really do love you, and you don't have to be perfect to be perfect for me.

George: Thanks, Deb. That means a lot to me. A lot of times I'd lead prayer or scriptures and I felt like you were telling me I was doing it all wrong. I just kind of got to the point where I didn't feel like I could do anything right.

Debbie: Wow. I didn't realize that was the case, but I believe you. I'll definitely do better in the future.

This was a great example because both were willing to open up about their concerns, and Debbie did a great job at supporting George who was likely struggling with his self-esteem and value as a priesthood holder. Debbie saw that it was more than just George who needed to change if they were to grow as a couple.

There are also cases when the pain and effect of one spouse's actions becomes unbearable. Feeling shamed, criticized, or attacked, or thinking that nothing you do will ever be enough for your spouse feels like a noose around the neck. Therapy and visits with your spiritual leader may be in store if you feel that your marriage or yourself, are beyond repair. Whichever route you choose, know that the incredibly healing power of the Atonement extends beyond the forgiveness of your sins. It offers you the power to forgive others because it is designed to pay the price for all people's sins as they come unto Him. As you seek for that power, you will feel a sense of dignity and positivity entering your life.

This doesn't mean that you simply have to be a victim of your spouse's transgressions. The Atonement can give you a sense of respect for yourself in that you learn of your own worth—not in a selfish or egotistical way or with a sense of entitlement—but simply in the fact that you will know that you are a child of God, that you have value, and that you deserve a marriage that is faithful. God never said anyone deserved a marriage that was "perfect," but we do know that we cannot become perfect without our spouses.

The Atonement can give you a sense of respect for yourself in that you learn of your own worth—not in a selfish or egotistical way or with a sense of entitlement—but simply in the fact that you will know that you have value.

As you accept the Atonement, you will also recognize the value in your spouse. Both of you are children of God. If you have been wronged by your parents, it may also be worthwhile to ask God to help you accept your parents more fully as human beings, with their strengths and weaknesses. If your parents abused or neglected you, plead to the Lord to help you focus on your spouse's strengths instead of believing your spouse will automatically be like your parents.

We typically do not feel the full effect of the Atonement until we have made significant changes in our thoughts and behavior. One of the most powerful techniques for learning to appreciate your spouse is keeping a gratitude journal and looking for the good in your spouse.

If you are in a difficult marriage, if you are the only spouse in your marriage willing to read and apply this book, or if you go to church or to therapy to help your marriage, realize that does not necessarily mean that your spouse is evil or less committed to your marriage. Some people feel particularly sensitive to discussing their marriages or how to improve them because they feel that bringing up marriage issues will cause more conflict. Sometimes this can be true.

As an analogy, there was a man who was told there were several holes in his garden. He didn't really see any, but he felt that other people could see the holes, so he spent hours and days trying to find the holes to fill. Unfortunately, the man was never done filling the holes in his garden because the dirt that filled one hole came from ground that was perfectly fine.

Similarly, when our focus is on fixing our spouse, our marriage, or even ourselves, we sometimes overlook the good things that already exist. Our focus is so much on change that we lose appreciation for what we have, never feeling satisfied because our lives with our spouses seems common, boring, or ordinary. The reality is that we are all usually doing the best with what we know how to do at the moment, and this holds true for our spouses too.

When we focus on fixing our spouse, we can overlook the good that already exists.

If you or your spouse has violated your covenants, you will need the help of the Lord. I understand why some might hesitate to share their burden, feel ashamed, or wonder how others will feel about them, but the reality is that you deserve help. Remember the boundaries discussed before. Never go to a friend or colleague of the opposite sex to discuss your troubles with your marriage. It may feel good but it will likely further weaken the boundaries within your marriage. However an exception to this may be sharing your concerns with church leaders or a parent. Again, consider the rules and their impact, and prayerfully ask to know what is right.

Regardless of your marital situation, do your best to feel the Spirit, especially when it seems hardest to do so. Plead for the Atonement and for the Holy Ghost to give you impressions on what to do for your marriage. Never let go of your relationship with God, and seek for guidance in all you do in your marriage.

Each of us can change, sometimes for the better and sometimes for the worse. Perhaps that is what is meant by "for better or worse," because we'll see our share of both versions in ourselves—and in our spouses.

RECOMMENDATIONS FOR KEEPING THE LORD IN YOUR MARRIAGE

1. Incorporate spiritual activities as part of your life and interaction with your spouse.

2. Understand that the Lord may be speaking to you but that your pain may make it difficult for you to hear Him. Try your best to reduce that pain by engaging in healthy interactions with others, having fun, taking up hobbies, and smiling.

3. Realize that you are entitled to all of the blessings Heavenly

Father has promised you if you keep your covenants, regardless of whether your spouse chooses to do the same.

4. Get help. Prayerfully consider who you should talk to, and who you shouldn't talk to, about serious issues in your marriage. Prayer, counseling, and friends can help you to restore your hope and dignity.

QUESTIONS TO PONDER AND ACTIVITIES TO CONSIDER

1. How do you treat your spouse? Please think about this question rather than discussing it right now. Actively think about how you treat your spouse. Ask yourself if how you treat your spouse is affected by how others have hurt you. Commit to a plan for improving how your treat your spouse.

2. Keep a Gratitude Journal, actively seeking for things you appreciate about your spouse. Avoid comparing your spouse to others or to what you think an ideal spouse should be like.

3. Seek for answers from the scriptures and in prayer. Consider how difficulties sometimes make it harder to seek the Lord. What will you do in those situations?

4. Prayerfully ask the Lord to make you less sensitive to your spouse's behaviors that cause you pain and ask Him to help you focus on the positive in your own life.

5. How do you feel about counseling? If you do seek counseling, prayerfully consider whether the therapist you are meeting with has your same values about the importance of marriage.

12

Boundaries of Expectations and Perfectionism

Expectations serve as powerful boundaries in marriage. When set and maintained properly, they say, "I believe in you more than anyone else." When used poorly, they say, "I don't believe in you, nor do I appreciate who you are." We learned earlier in this book that expectations are healthy for our marriage, as long as they are fair. Years ago, while completing my dissertation on married parents, I found that our expectations for our spouses often lead to reality. In my dissertation, I noted that fathers tended to be more involved in the lives of their children when mothers had high expectations for their husbands *even before their baby was born.*

Expectations for your spouse, when set appropriately, serve as a guide for telling your spouse what you feel is important for a successful relationship. Because your spouse loves you and you love your spouse, each of you will try to live up to the potential you see in each other. Put simply, I am a better husband and father because of the expectations my wife has for me.

While expectations can serve as a motivation for improving relationships, they can also be a catalyst for frustration. When expectations are perceived as unfair

or too high or when they are interpreted as ingratitude or manipulation, conflict is born.

When we get married, we probably see our spouses as perfect, or close to it, but after living with them we quickly recognize their faults and weaknesses. It is a little like having a perfect garden or lawn, and then watching a huge weed grow in the middle of it. It is easy to focus on the imperfection, rather than the beauty that dominates the landscape.

Another problem with expectations can arise when one spouse expects the other to offset any and all weaknesses that the first spouse's parents had. "My mother and father never cared about me, so you've got to prove to me that you do." This may not be directly expressed, but the emotion or subconscious power of that statement is nonetheless real. If you have been hurt in this or a similar way by your parents, realize that you likely have a tendency to focus on any similarities between your spouse and the parent(s) who hurt you, which will limit your positive appraisals of your spouse. Sometimes a caring spouse will try to compensate for the other spouse's neglectful childhood, doing everything he or she can but always feeling judged or like they are not enough. The reality is that no one can go back to the past and change what has already been done, and when one spouse focuses on the past then their present and past become distorted. They are less grateful because all they see is their own pain instead of seeing their spouse for who he or she really is.

Another common experience related to harmful expectations is when one spouse expects help but feels smarter or more responsible for a certain task. It's common to hear of husbands taking care of a baby, loading the dishes, or doing the laundry, and then becoming frustrated because they're told they didn't do it right or didn't do it well enough. Some wives may even shame their husbands for their attempt. In general, when men receive this type of treatment they will either get outwardly angry or withdraw emotionally or physically from the relationship.

Similarly, I know of women who have felt that they were "never enough" for their husbands and that regardless of what they did, they could not reach a level of acceptance from their husbands. For some their house wasn't clean enough. For others their employment didn't pay enough or it paid too much—earning them more than their husband's job. And still others did not feel that their husbands thought they were pretty.

The danger point for crossing from healthy to unhealthy expectations occurs when your sense of value is completely dependent on whether your spouse meets those expectations. Does your self-esteem fluctuate based on what your spouse earns? Do you feel different about yourself based upon how your spouse dresses? Do you feel threatened if your spouse does a better job at a certain task than you do or if your spouse has talents that exceed your own?

Perfectionist attitudes or expectations toward your spouse often develop because you see the imperfections in yourself. More specifically, if you are a perfectionist, it is likely that you do not accept the faults in yourself and do your best to develop a sense of control by controlling others. Ironically, the very thing you wish to have for yourself—acceptance—is what you deny your spouse. But you can change.

Another danger for expectations is when one spouse expects the other to mess up or fall short. Spouses who adopt this attitude feel they have been let down or they don't want to be hurt if their spouse doesn't meet their more positive expectations.

If you suspect one of these descriptions might fit you, I recommend you review everything you can about forgiveness, whether you are the one with harmful expectations or the recipient of those expectations. Therapy and talking with your spiritual leader can be helpful.

Here are a few warning signs to watch for that suggest control and manipulation with regard to expectations:

- Do you criticize your spouse for not making a choice or for not behaving a certain way, and then, when they try to improve, do you continue to criticize them for not doing it well enough or in the way you think is right?

- Does your spouse get frustrated that your standard for what is "good enough" seems to change?

- Do you get angry when your spouse doesn't do what you want, and then become happy and rewarding when they do?
- Do you become incredibly nice after being confronted for controlling behavior, but then quickly revert to being dissatisfied with your spouse's behaviors?
- Do you frequently find yourself feeling that your spouse does not love you for not doing things a certain way?

The more you answered "yes" to these question, the more likely it is that controlling or manipulative behaviors are present in you and your relationship. I believe that being able to accept Christ's Atonement is central to being able to get past controlling behavior. Learn to recognize what He wants you to be and realize His power is sufficient to make you that way. Forgiving yourself and your spouse for your wrongs is necessary in order to move on and improve.

If you are the victim in this kind of a relationship, be honest with yourself and look at your own behaviors to determine if you have contributed to the situation. This can be difficult and painful because when you feel you have been deeply hurt, you will be especially wary of following certain rules, fearing you will only be hurt more or trampled on again. Following the principles in this book will give you a good start for talking about boundaries, including issues of unequal power and controlling behaviors. Ask yourself if you have encouraged your spouse to take over or take control. Perhaps you have shown a reluctance to make decisions or have given your spouse a cause to not believe in you. You may also want to consider how your childhood influenced your perceptions of gender, power, and relationships.

Sometimes we expect our spouses to meet all of our emotional needs. Certainly, our spouses should meet as many emotional needs as possible, but we cross the line when our sense of value becomes completely determined by how our spouse acts and talks to us and others. That is when our jealousy can become controlling.

Taking accountability for your part, whether great or small, is the first and a very courageous step for developing power, influence, self-respect, and self-control. Those who are "angry silent" may perpetuate a sense of control over their spouse that their spouse can see but they cannot.

> **Taking accountability for your part, whether great or small, is the first and a courageous step for developing power, influence, self-respect, and self-control.**

I want to be clear that these recommendations are about general conflict, which occurs among most marriages; no one ever deserves to be abused! It is possible that, if you are the recipient of these behaviors, you have honestly done all you can. If this is you, you will need professional help to maintain your dignity, your self-respect, and your marriage.

For now, let's look at a couple examples for talking about perfectionism, manipulation, and controlling behaviors.

Christine: Doug, do you have a minute for us to talk about something important to me?

Doug: I'm pretty busy. What's up?

Christine: I understand you are busy, so we can talk later. But this is something that is really important to me and to our marriage. When would be better?

Doug: Oh. I didn't realize it was that important. Well, definitely, let's talk about it now.

Christine: Doug, this is really painful for me to talk about, so at first I just need you to listen to me. I really need my voice to be heard.

Doug: Of course, honey, but when do you listen to me?

Christine: If I've hurt you by not listening to you, I want to apologize right now. I'd like to share what I have to say and then I want you to let me know how I can do better.

Doug: What's come over you? You're getting a little bossy.

Christine: Doug, please know that I love you and want to be with you forever. I am forever yours and I want you to know that I'll do everything within my power to help make this home and your life as comfortable as possible. Unfortunately, for several years I have felt unappreciated, unloved, and that I am not good enough. I need you to let me know, constantly, that I *am* good enough. I don't expect you to be perfect and I need to know that you are okay with me making mistakes, learning, and growing. Our marriage needs to be a safe place, and I see you as my protector. I need your protection by accepting me for me.

Doug: I really didn't know you felt that way. Why didn't you see anything before?

Christine: I tried, and perhaps I didn't say it in the right way. But I'd like to focus on the here and now and what we can do to improve our marriage. I need you to protect me, and the way to do that is by accepting me. I need you to tell me I'm pretty, that you appreciate my income from work, and that I'm a good parent. I need those words and I deeply need you. You are incredible, and I need that incredibleness to help me heal.

Doug: I'm really sorry I hurt you, love. You definitely are beautiful, and I appreciate all your efforts and talents. I'm sorry I haven't been supportive, or at least haven't given you the type of support you have needed. Can we keep talking about this? Because I honestly do not recognize when I am being that way to you,

That exchange started out difficult because it was clear that Doug did not respect Christine the way he should. While we should never condone his actions, it is important to again understand that his history may have contributed to those actions. Christine did a good job of standing her ground, telling Doug it was important, and being clear without using accusatory labels when she could have said something like, "Stop being controlling." She also appealed to the power that her husband needed, by asking him to be her protector, but tried to channel that power in a way that would help the marriage.

It's also important to recognize that it isn't always men who are controlling. My point is not to place blame on a particular gender or create gender wars but to help us understand that conflict often comes from an imbalance of power rather than from a particular gender. Let's turn it around and see what this conversation might look like if Doug was the one who felt that Christine was being controlling.

Doug: Hi, love. I need a few minutes for us to talk about something that is very important to me and our marriage.

Christine: Oh, honey. There's always something else about me that you think I need to change.

Doug: I'm sorry if I've hurt you in any way; I will take responsibility for that. Let's talk about that after I share my thoughts, okay?

Christine: That's okay. What did you want to talk about?

Doug: Well, first, going back to what you said, because I want you to know how you feel is important to me . . . You're right, I'm concerned about how I'm treated. When I try to do the right thing, I feel I am criticized, yelled at, or shamed—both in private and public.

Christine: I just think you're being oversensitive.

Doug: Maybe, and maybe I need to get help for that. But marriage is about having each other's back. When people ask me about you or say how awesome you are, I have your back and don't tell them of the pain I feel. When they say how wonderful you are and how many talents you have, I feel invisible to them, but I don't tell them about the years I took care of you when you were struggling with your diet and depression. And when they say how kind you are, I don't tell them that I go to bed crying because you tell other men how wonderful they are and most of the time I feel criticized or shamed.

Christine: I'm sorry you feel that way.

Doug: Christine, if the tables were switched, do you know how many women would come to the aid for you? And yet, because I'm a man, I'm judged differently. I'm a wimp, or worse, and I feel guilty and ashamed even bringing this up. But I need help, and I need your help. You have incredible talents, I know, and I need you to share them with me. I need to know that you love, respect, and admire me, and that you are committed to me more than anyone else. Instead, you criticize me for what I say and then start talking over me. Or I try to help you and I'm criticized. I'm tired of you saying "Thanks for trying." I need to be enough, and honestly, I'd like to be the most important person in the world to you.

Christine: I honestly don't see the same thing that you see, but I love you and want you to know that you are the most important— and the *only*—person in the world for me. I want to share forever with you, and I'm sorry I've hurt you. What kinds of things would help you feel like the most important person to me?

This interaction also started roughly, as those who are controlling will often deflect any responsibility for pain onto another person. It is also possible that those who engage in controlling behavior genuinely do not see themselves as controlling. But, like the earlier example, Doug was clear about what he needed while limiting potentially disparaging remarks. Often, what happens in these situations is that the victim in the relationship will try to assert control, in the same way his or her spouse did in the past, but clearly two negatives do not make a positive. Christine also apologized and sought for ways to show Doug in his own language and way, that he was the most important person in the world to him.

QUESTIONS TO PONDER AND ACTIVITIES TO CONSIDER

1. How do your expectations influence your perception of your marriage?

2. Are your expectations for your spouse or marriage fair and realistic?

3. Are your expectations for yourself fair and realistic?

4. At what point do expectations move from helpful to hurtful?

5. Write down the expectations that you have for your spouse. After that, consider whether those expectations have hurt or strengthened your spouse and relationship. Question why you have certain expectations. After that, write the expectations you have for yourself and see how they have either strengthened or hurt you and your relationship. Determine what to do about your future expectations.

CONCLUSION

Throughout this book, we have learned how certain boundaries can bring couples together. We have also learned how other boundaries can divide spouses. As mentioned early in the book, I think one of the biggest opportunities—and sometimes one of the biggest challenges—is to show your spouse that you love them with all your heart. Your spouse should have your closest affection and proximity, your kindest words and forgiveness, and your greatest time and focus. Boundaries often need to be adjusted because of past experiences, cultural beliefs, and the current needs of each spouse.

Several times throughout this book, you and your spouse have been encouraged to decide which boundaries are and are not for your marriage. Take each of the recommendations with a grain—or cup—of salt, depending on where your marriage is and what it needs. Only you and your spouse can say for sure what you need as a couple.

But once you agree on certain boundaries, it's a good idea to discuss them often, with the focus on what you know about boundaries, namely that you want to use them to protect and strengthen your relationship with your spouse. You want your marriage to grow by leaps and boundaries. Avoid forcing your spouse to agree with you, since that alone creates boundaries. Remember to use the Atonement daily, to ask for your own forgiveness and, when needed, to help you forgive your spouse.

Creating and maintaining proper boundaries in marriage is a never-ending process. Some couples are better at it than others. It's okay if everything isn't "just so."

Believe in yourself and in your spouse. And believe that God wants your marriage to be fulfilling for both you and your spouse.

Reread what you need to in this book and skip what you don't want to read. But keep your understanding that maintaining boundaries within your marriage and between your marriage and others will help the two of you foster greater trust in, loyalty to, respect for, admiration for, and belief in each other—when done the right way.

Always remember that the goal of forming boundaries is not to isolate yourself or your marriage but to defend your relationship from those things that can hurt it. Little things can hurt your marriage, and little things can also heal it.

Try to focus on the positive and celebrate the good in your marriage. Focus on the little things. For me, one of those little things was meatloaf.

The first time I made meatloaf, I basically threw in everything I could think of—or at least everything that was available. I knew that meat was required, but beyond that I really did not know what else was supposed to be in a meatloaf. I had seasoned crackers, molasses, celery, dried mustard powder, oil, sour cream, and oregano. So that's what I put into the meat. Then I threw it in the oven for approximately 30 minutes at 400 degrees.

Admittedly, I was surprised at how good it tasted, but the real test was whether my wife would like it. Fortunately for me, I got an A grade and now she brags about my meatloaf all the time and asks me when I'm going to cook it again. I love making her meatloaf.

A successful marriage is about simple things—just like a meatloaf. You take what you have and do your best with those things to make your spouse happy. Each time, like my own undocumented recipe, it will likely turn out a little differently. But in the end you'll have something worth cheering over.

I was worried to eat it, to be honest with you. It didn't look great, and I like my food great. It smelled great though. When I ate it, it tasted great, and was surprised with how great it was. Each time he makes it, it looks different. But it still tastes great. I agree it's the small things in marriage, like cooking, influences how we feel about our marriage. (A note from Sarah, Jerry's wife).

APPENDIX A

Review of Chapters

INTRODUCTION

Review

Boundaries determine where the line is drawn as far as what is appropriate, acceptable, and preferred in your marriage. Boundaries are important because they help a couple share common ground, build trust, and commit to each other more. Not knowing where the boundaries are or having different ideas of where those boundaries are placed, leads to frustration, confusion, and conflict.

Many couples may not have the tools, strategies, or words they need to discuss boundaries. This creates weaker marriages. Knowing how to manage and negotiate the boundaries in your marriage will make it stronger.

Ponder

1. What rules, expectations, and practices did I learn about boundaries with others while I was growing up?

2. What boundaries did my parents encourage me to maintain? Was my parents' marriage the most important relationship to them? How did their example influence my own expectations about marriage and boundaries?

3. What safeguards does the world have for protecting my marriage? What safeguards does my community, background, or church offer for protecting my marriage?

4. Do my spouse and I know what boundaries exist within our marriage? Do we agree on how to treat each other and how to interact with others?

Apply

Boundary maintenance is best done with the cooperation of both spouses. However, if your spouse is not interested in addressing boundary issues, realize that your spouse has his or her agency. Your spouse may not be interested in discussing boundary issues because he or she is afraid of hurting your feelings. Have you shown the ability to listen? Have you been supportive and not defensive?

Start by considering your role in boundary formation. Practice by taking accountability for your actions, rather than blaming others (including your spouse). Pray for the guidance of the Holy Ghost to direct your behavior in a way that will allow you to accept your spouse for their talents and efforts.

Study the scriptures to identify boundaries that may be particularly useful for you and your marriage. Be clear with yourself that you will not manipulate your spouse into changing. Instead you will take accountability for yourself and how you impact the marriage relationship—for better and for worse.

CHAPTER 1: THE BENEFITS OF MARRIAGE

Review

History and research have shown that married individuals tend to experience greater health and wealth and a better social life. It is important for each couple to determine why marriage is important to them in order to have the proper motivation for creating and maintaining boundaries to protect their marriage.

Ponder

1. How do I feel that marriage benefits society as a whole?
2. In what ways do I benefit from being married?

Apply

Consider writing a note or poem to your spouse, letting your spouse know why you appreciate him or her and how he or she benefit your life.

CHAPTER 2: WHY BOUNDARIES ARE IMPORTANT

Review

Boundaries are largely determined by our attitudes and expectations. Generally speaking, having high expectations for your marriage is a good thing, because it encourages you and your spouse to have a high-functioning marriage. Marriages tend to live up to the spouses' expectations and standards.

Ponder

1. We draw boundaries when we determine our priorities. In what ways do I make my marriage more important than other relationships?

2. What do boundaries do for a marriage? How can they bring a married couple together and how can they divide spouses?

3. Do I have high expectations or standards for my marriage?

Apply

Now is a good time to visit with your spouse about boundaries. Realize that the application or negotiation of boundaries is largely determined by our own childhood experiences and observations.

Write down your expectations for your marriage. Are they high expectations? Are they realistic expectations? Are your expectations for your marriage, your spouse, or yourself unfair or unrealistic?

Discuss with your spouse the different reasons why each of you married. This will help you understand what expectations each of you had for the marriage. This is not a time to blame or criticize, and if it turns into a source of contention, agree to leave it alone and just to consider individually how your own expectations influence your behavior and reactions to your spouse.

CHAPTER 3: PHYSICAL BOUNDARIES

Review

Physical boundaries have to do with how close you position your body to your spouse and to others, how much affection and intimacy the two of you offer each other, how much affection you give to others (especially those of the opposite sex), and the clothes you wear.

You can determine where these boundaries are by understanding your own comfort level in these areas and your spouse's preferences, and by ensuring that your behavior is consistent with gospel standards. A person's preferences for physical boundaries can be influenced by childhood experiences, biological predispositions, the media, community standards, and abuse.

Boundary creation and maintenance is fueled by acceptance and appreciation from both spouses for each other. Each spouse should try to understand the perspective of the other, and thereby show respect and a willingness to negotiate boundary adherence. Talking about physical boundaries can feel uncomfortable for many spouses, particularly if they have not had a successful experience with those discussions in the past.

Gender differences also influence the level of comfort one feels toward certain expressions of affection, proximity, and clothing—both in private and in public. It is important be aware of these differences to safeguard your marriage.

Ponder

1. What beliefs do I have about physical boundaries? When am I comfortable with how my spouse treats me? When am I uncomfortable with how my spouse interacts with others?

2. Are my present beliefs about affection, both toward my spouse and to others, consistent with gospel standards?

3. Have I considered how I interact with the opposite sex, and whether my spouse is comfortable with how I treat and am treated by the opposite sex?

4. Have I considered how my appearance or clothing might impact others, including how my spouse feels in private and in public?

5. Do I show my spouse that I feel closer to him or her than any other person? Am I physically closer to my spouse than to others I am around? Do I show more affection to my spouse than to members of the opposite sex? Do my clothing and actions represent my loyalty to my spouse and none other?

Apply

Consider taking one boundary concern or issue at a time, rather than trying to tackle all of them at once. This is not a race! Remember that the main purpose of boundaries is to bring the partners in a marriage together. Attempting to compel change in your spouse can actually weaken your marriage. Show respect, love, and appreciation for your spouse regardless of whether he or she conforms to what you feel is the best way. Remember that there are many options but do take accountability for how your own actions compare to gospel standards.

If you and your spouse choose to talk about physical boundaries, use words that reaffirm your loyalty to, appreciation for, and admiration of your spouse regardless of the outcome of that discussion. Look to understand your spouse's perspective and make sure you both have a voice in determining where the boundaries ought to be.

If possible, discuss what affection, proximity, and intimacy mean to each of you and to your marriage. Recognize that differences will likely exist and it is important that neither spouse feels judged for those feelings. Remember that true boundary formation and maintenance can only occur when your focus is on each other and your marriage, and not on the problems. Be a problem-solver not a problem-maker. Make certain you each feel loved and not criticized.

CHAPTER 4: VERBAL AND EMOTIONAL BOUNDARIES

Review

Verbal and emotional boundaries, like physical boundaries, represent how close you feel to your spouse and your marriage. They should show that you think of, respect, and admire your spouse more than any other person. A great deal of temptation can be circumvented by filling your spouse's emotional tank.

Avoid dialogues about being someone else's spouse, even if you're only joking. During times of difficulty, those seeds grow into dangerous weeds, even when the conversations initially seemed harmless. Consider how direct compliments to the opposite sex and complaining about your spouse in public impact your marriage. Conversely, consider the impact of direct compliments to and verbal admiration for your spouse. Realize that boundaries, and the formation of them, may mean something different to you than they do to your spouse. Be willing to accept, negotiate, and uphold the boundaries that are important for you and your spouse. Whether at work, at church, or with youth, the boundaries you set will be interpreted in a certain way. Youth are especially uncertain of boundaries, and it's important that you set a good example for them.

Ponder

1. Is it possible that my words about and to my spouse (in public and in private) are hurting our marriage? Have I considered my tone as well as my words?

2. Does my spouse crave positive words from me?

3. Am I showing, through my words and my actions, that my spouse is more important to me than anyone else?

4. Do I agree with the assumption that we should limit direct compliments to members of the opposite sex? Why or why not?

5. Are there things that I say, either because I think they're funny or needed for correction, that end up limiting our marriage potential?

Apply

Consider recording yourself or at least writing down everything you say to and about your spouse. Try this for at least a couple days. Consider whether your conversations have been normal or if you have altered your language simply because you are watching yourself. If you suspect you have been speaking better than you usually do, consider recording yourself more often. Remember that the recording or writing down of your comments is meant to help you improve your verbal comments and not to flatter your ego. Be honest with yourself.

Think about altering how you communicate with the opposite sex. Are you often giving compliments, such as "You're awesome," "You're so funny," or "You're incredible"? If you changed your approach or compliments to be indirect ("That was awesome, funny, or incredible"), how would it impact your marriage relationship and your willingness to be more personal with your compliments to your spouse? Conversely, keep a record of how many times you show appreciation for ("thank you for . . .") and give direct compliments to your spouse.

If needed, pray for guidance on how to negotiate verbal boundaries with your spouse. Keep in mind that boundaries are designed to strengthen your marriage but if mishandled they can hurt that relationship. Consider lessons in the scriptures about how verbal and emotional boundaries can help or hurt a marriage.

CHAPTER 5: SOCIAL RELATIONSHIPS AND NETWORKING

Review

Friendships and family relationships are incredibly important to our well-being. However, their importance does not supersede the importance the Lord has placed on marriage relationships.

Overstepping boundaries can include seeking financial advice from someone outside your marriage, giving personal information about your spouse to someone you shouldn't, or going online frequently or in secret to converse with or check up on former boyfriends or girlfriends. Always ask yourself if your spouse would approve of the way in which you share or seek information and how much you do share.

Ponder

1. Do I only share personal information when my spouse would feel comfortable with me doing so?

2. Do I value my spouse's values and beliefs more than I value those of other people?

3. Do I sincerely believe that my marriage relationship takes priority over all other relationships? Why or why not?

Apply

Evaluate the friends you have or want to have. Consider whether those friends share your beliefs about marriage boundaries and what pressures you would experience if you continued in or made those friendships.

If you have recently crossed the line or a boundary with regard to sharing information about any personal matter, ask for forgiveness from your spouse. If the person you shared that information with asks you to share more with them, politely but firmly explain that you should not have crossed that boundary and that you have chosen to be more selective about the information you share in the future. Be clear that you still value their friendship but that you felt what you shared was inappropriate. Be clear that this is your decision and not something your spouse is making you do.

When you are around your friends and people you network with, practice talking more about your spouse and what you admire about your spouse. Go through the last two weeks' worth of comments you made online or via text to see what you wrote about your spouse and how you can improve. Avoid gossip sessions or people who try to pry negative information about your spouse from you. Recognize how your words and boundaries, whether online or in public, might be interpreted by others as saying that you do not feel close to your spouse.

CHAPTER 6: THE MEDIA

Review

How much media each spouse watches, when they watch, whether they watch alone, and what they watch—especially if it's something the other spouse is uncomfortable with—can increase the boundaries *between* couples. Watching TV or a movie is not a bad thing, even if you are watching by yourself, but there is a point when a person's desire for watching TV or surfing the Internet becomes more important than his or her spouse's needs.

The brain is a survival organ, which means it tends to store information, especially images that have high emotional value, positive or negative. When a person feels stressed, the brain retrieves information on how to deal with the situation. So if a person watches a lot of negative media images, then those negative thoughts will eventually become hardwired into a person's response to stress.

Ponder

1. How much media am I watching or listening to? Does this tally include TV, movies, the Internet, and music?

2. What percentage of the media that I watch or listen to has at least one message counter to my beliefs about marriage or love?

3. Do I place media consumption over things that ought to be more important in my life?

4. Do my spouse and I use the media as a resource for bringing us together or does it tend to divide us?

Apply

Keep a record of how much media you consume, at least during non-work hours. If possible, write down what positive and what negative messages you view or listen to. Consider spending less time with the media and more time strengthening your marriage. If you feel dependent on the media, seek to replace those habits with hobbies, wholesome entertainment, and time spent with family and friends.

CHAPTER 7: FINANCES AND EMPLOYMENT

Review

Finances may be the most common argument in marriages. This is because, unlike affection, once money is spent, it is gone. Financial arguments or disagreements over what is best or most appropriate with regard to financial boundaries usually focus on how much money is or should be saved and how to spend money. It's important that money be used to strengthen a marriage and not to tear it apart. Remember that the money you earn belongs to both of you, although you and your spouse may choose to designate a specific amount for each spouse to spend independently.

It's also important to understand how *not* to talk about money.

Talking about how little a father brings in is damaging to his worth and sense of purpose. Being critical of a wife who is or isn't employed adds to the incredible pressure and mixed messages women today receive about their eternal identity. Remember to not speak critically of a spouse who may not be the best at fulfilling traditional roles, such as being a good mechanic or cook. Avoid asking for outside help with roles that your spouse feels responsible for, unless your spouse feels comfortable with that help.

It's important to know what your boundaries are and what your spouse's boundaries are when employed. This is especially true about interacting with the opposite sex. Do not share anything with a coworker, especially one of the opposite sex, that your spouse would feel uncomfortable about. When there are situations where your work requires you to cross a boundary, make sure your spouse is the first person to know about it.

Ponder

1. Am I ever critical of how my spouse contributes financially? If so, how can I change?

2. Do I ask others for help when I know my spouse would disapprove? If so, how can I change?

3. Would any of my interactions with colleagues make my spouse uncomfortable?

4. If situations come up at work that I know my spouse would feel uncomfortable with, is he or she the first to know about them?

5. What financial boundaries work for our marriage? Which ones may need to be revised or improved upon?

Apply

There are many aspects of financial boundaries. Reflect back on the last week or keep a record this week of how you talk to and about your spouse regarding his or her financial roles, talents, or limitations. Discuss what different financial roles or responsibilities mean to each of you.

Review the chapter on financial boundaries if you need some strategies and words to discuss or negotiate financial boundaries. Discuss with your spouse what boundaries need to exist between your marriage and others regarding seeking financial advice, sharing financial information (including how much money you make), and asking others for help that relates to a spouse's abilities or role.

CHAPTER 8: BEING PARENTS

Review

Being the kinds of parents God would want us to be is a solemn responsibility. Our children are dependent on us for so many things, including helping them develop their own testimonies. However, it's important to recognize that our marriages still need to be the most important relationships we have, and it is important for our children to see healthy marriages.

Be as close to your children as you can, but not in a way that competes with or isolates your spouse from your children. Realize that children often serve as natural boundaries between you and others, but be careful that you do not place that burden directly upon them.

Ponder

1. Am I the kind of parent God would want me to be?

2. Do my children know that I adore, admire, and love my spouse—even more than them?

3. Do I believe that marriage is the most important relationship a person should have?

4. Do I ever use my children as boundaries between me and situations or people I am uncomfortable with?

Apply

Seek for opportunities to show your gratitude, respect, and love for your spouse in front of your children. Be clear that marriage is the most important relationship they could ever have and try to be a good example of this so they feel this the case with you. Be alert to ways that you use your children as boundaries and determine whether those ways are appropriate or not. Consider your heart and your actions and whether these things impact how your children feel toward your spouse.

CHAPTER 9: SOME BOUNDARIES FOR EACH STAGE OF MARRIAGE

Review

Recently being married and the age of your child represent critical moments for implementing boundaries. Newlyweds experience intense highs, but they may also have very difficult moments, which serves as an opportunity (and a challenge) for determining what boundaries should exist. Having a child, and that child getting older, can serve as a boundary between spouses or can serve as a boundary that protects the marriage.

Ponder

1. What expectations can the two of you agree upon?
2. How much time should you and your child spend together? How do you spend "enough" time with your spouse?
3. What level of affection is appropriate in public?
4. How will you show your child that you are loyal to your spouse? How will you show your child of your love while being clear of your first loyalty to your spouse?

Apply

As a couple, consider the needs and wants of your child(ren), then talk about how they can be met, if possible, while still giving the time, energy, and other resources needed to sustain your marriage. Tell each other what your favorite things are about being a parent. If you are not parents yet, talk about what joys and challenges you anticipate, and how you will approach resolving those challenges.

CHAPTER 10: BOUNDARIES OF ROLES AND RESPONSIBILITIES

Review

Contrary to many songs and myths, love does not conquer all. It acts as a motivator, guide, and boundary, but there is a time when you and your spouse must decide who does the dishes, takes out the trash, takes your child to the doctor, and so on.

Our society is rapidly changing, and each new generation is, in part, left to figure out on its own how to reconcile what society expects of them with the realities of their own marriages. Be willing to revise roles and responsibilities when needed; avoid territorial or martyrlike assignments.

Ponder

1. What roles do I believe women and men should have with regard to employment, housework, parenting, and other responsibilities? How are my values or perceptions about these roles shaped by tradition?

2. Are my beliefs about roles and responsibilities in marriage consistent with gospel teachings?

3. Why are boundaries, rules, and expectations for roles and responsibilities meaningful to me? How can I ensure that my own beliefs about roles and responsibilities do not hurt but instead strengthen my marriage?

4. Am I willing to negotiate or to accept a role or responsibility I wouldn't typically think should be mine?

5. Do I view my spouse's roles and responsibilities in the same way as my spouse does? For example, how does my spouse view doing dishes or being employed?

Apply

Consider the characteristics, talents, and beliefs that you each have acquired from your childhood experiences. Discuss how roles and responsibilities for men and women have changed over the last few decades.

Now that you understand that childhood backgrounds, socioeconomic circumstances, and other factors influence your and your spouse's values about roles and responsibilities, talk about what the roles in your marriage mean to each of you? The goal is *not* to seek out differences but to better understand how each role or responsibility affects your spouse—and how to help your spouse with his or her own understanding of those roles.

CHAPTER 11: SPIRITUAL BOUNDARIES

Review

While the church we attend can be a great source of guidance on spiritual and marital matters, it can also place a great deal of pressure on both spouses to be perfect. You or your spouse may feel a need to be the perfect wife or the perfect husband. Or the perfect mother. Or the best breadwinner.

While the spiritual checklists, with questions like "Did I say my prayers?" and "Did I read my scriptures?" can be helpful to make sure you are on track, we must realize that the Savior offered himself because he knew we would not be perfect in this lifetime. He knew that we could only become perfect with His Atonement. Be careful not to judge yourself or your spouse too harshly if he or she does not fit the ideal image of a parent or spouse in the church. That was never a requirement for receiving all of God's blessings.

Ponder

1. Do I allow the Atonement and mercy of Christ to offset my own weaknesses and to help me forgive my spouse when needed?

2. Do I have unfair expectations for my spouse's spirituality? How does that impact our relationship?

3. Do I ever criticize my spouse about his or her spirituality?

4. Do I see more good in our relationship, and in the spirit that upholds our relationship, than I see weaknesses?

Apply

Seek for the guidance of the Holy Ghost to comfort and direct you in your marriage. Look for the blessings of the Atonement by giving yourself permission to accept the Atonement for your own weaknesses and those of your spouse. Constantly identify more positives about your spouse's spirituality and show your gratitude to your spouse and to God for those strengths.

CHAPTER 12: BOUNDARIES OF EXPECTATIONS AND PERFECTIONISM

Review

Having high expectations for one's spouse and oneself is healthy when those expectations are motivational, strengthening, and seem to say, "I believe in you." They are harmful when they are critical, degrading, and seem to ask, "What's wrong with you?" Harmful expectations often evolve from a sense of not being enough for your spouse or from difficult experiences in your past and a fear of getting hurt again.

Ponder

1. What expectations do I have for my spouse? How can I know if they are hurtful or harmful to our relationship?

2. Why do I have certain positive and negative expectations for my spouse? How can I overcome the negative expectations?

Apply

Review the chapter for information on how to forgive yourself and others, including your spouse. Write down what you have learned.

CHAPTER 13: CONCLUSION

Review

You have reviewed a great deal about boundaries in marriage! Give yourself, and your spouse, a break and don't expect perfection. Each of you has your own strengths and challenges for recognizing, creating, and maintaining boundaries. Remember that boundaries can either strengthen or hurt your marriage, and largely depend on how you and your spouse work together.

It may be helpful to periodically review the book, or sections of it, from time to time. Chances are high that time and experience will give you insight that will further increase your understanding for applying the principles of boundaries.

Ponder

1. What boundaries do you feel are most important in your marriage?

2. What are a few principles or themes you have found (either in this book or from your own experience) about spouses working together on boundaries?

3. How has your marriage improved by working on boundaries? What are some of the challenges with boundaries, and how can you show your spouse greater commitment through boundary creation and maintenance?

Apply

In a journal or diary, write down what you have learned about boundaries in marriage. Make a pledge for what you are committed to doing, and allow yourself the flexibility, if needed, to revisit your beliefs about boundaries if it will help further strengthen your marriage.

APPENDIX B

Dates Every Couple Can Do

- Late at night, before you go to bed, recite your marital vows to your spouse or write new ones.
- Give each other massages.
- Write a letter to your spouse telling them how they have inspired you in life.
- Read the scriptures together.
- Take a walk and talk about the different marital couples you admire—and why.
- Write little love notes and leave them everywhere around the house for your spouse.
- Cook your spouse's favorite dinner. If you have children, find a babysitter for them or if they are older or especially well-behaved, ask them if they'll serve you and your spouse.
- Write "I love you" in your spouse's food.
- Send an e-card telling your spouse why you love them.
- Sing karaoke together.

- Watch a video on your laptop together.
- Secretly offer a service project or snack to your neighbors and friends.
- Visit nursing or retirement centers together.
- Write a poem for your spouse.
- Fold a note of appreciation into your spouse's laundry or dresser drawers.
- Try to make up your own silly jokes or stories and share them with each other.
- Do research together on something you want to do (like taking a vacation or making a purchase).
- Play a game of Go Fish together.
- Go on a double date.
- Pretend you are introducing yourself to your spouse for the first time.
- Ask your spouse to dance with you in the kitchen.
- Write a note of appreciation for your spouse and send it to your spouse's parents.
- Play charades.
- Go on a picnic.
- Play the songs you enjoyed when the two of you met.
- Learn to play a musical instrument together.
- Go caroling.
- Create coupons for your spouse for things he or she will like or want.
- Draw a self-portrait with a crayon held between your toes.
- Hold each other on the couch and don't say anything.
- Tell your spouse the things about him or her that turn you on.
- Watch a really old movie.
- Create a short skit or play in which the two of you are the only actors.

- Write an original story you would like to see in one of your favorite TV shows.
- Dress up as your favorite superhero.
- Build paper airplanes.
- Create a building within nothing but toothpicks, glue, and paper.
- Write your own primary song.
- Talk about your favorite memories while looking through pictures of your wedding day.
- Learn sign language together.
- Write your congressman about the importance of a bill.
- Look through childhood pictures together.
- Take a picture and use editing software to alter it. Compare this process to how you ought to look at your marriage.
- Find a trampoline and jump on it.
- Take turns blindfolding and leading each other around a place that has special significance to your marriage.
- Chat with your spouse online.
- Discuss what movies you find most inspirational.
- Create a card for your spouse explaining what chances they took by marrying you.
- Describe your marriage using Twitter rules (140 characters or less).
- Give your spouse as many compliments as you can.
- Sing a love song to your spouse or karaoke if that would be more effective.
- Talk to each other as if you were two years old.
- Call your grandparents while you're both on the phone.
- Fill up the gas tank for your spouse.
- Clean out the car for your spouse.
- Get up early and make your spouse's favorite meal.

- Send a letter through the mail to your spouse.
- Shine your spouse's shoes.
- Iron your spouse's clothes.
- Learn a new recipe together.
- Put away the dishes together.
- Create your own maze or crossword puzzles together.
- Look at something and write down everything you see. Compare what the two of you have written down.
- Answer the following question: If you had a clone you could control, what would you have it do?
- Make cupcakes.
- Take a drive together for no particular reason.
- Create a face or figure on a paper bag and place it over your head. See if your spouse can guess who the face or figure is.
- Carve a jack-o-lantern.
- Spit watermelon seeds as far as you can.
- Share a popsicle.
- Compete to see who can clean a certain part of the house first.
- Nominate your spouse for a "Spouse of the Year" award.
- Leave "love note" voicemails for each other.
- Put together a few of your favorite tangible memories and deliver them to your spouse.
- Go to the thrift store and buy something for your spouse using three dollars or less.
- Every night, read scriptures together and then talk about how you can apply those scriptures in your marriage.
- Play hide-and-seek or go on a treasure hunt with another couple using a GPS device and coordinates.
- Read a fun book together.
- Recite the most memorable lines from inspirational or funny movies.

- In one minute, name all the foods you can think of that start with the letter "A." Continue through the letter "Z." Or if you don't want to name foods, pick any category you want.

- Sing one of your favorite songs as if it were in an opera.

- Stare at each other. See who can go the longest without smiling.

- Create your own (perhaps fictitious) organization or intervention that helps couples. What would it do? What would it look like?

- Watch *Chariots of Fire* and turn down the sound. Pretend you have written the script and act it out while the show is playing.

- Have your own talent show.

- Create your own version of American Idol and invite others over to participate.

- Create your own lemonade and, with two straws, share the drink.

- Go to the mall, sit on a bench, and hold hands. Count how many people look at you.

- Ask your spouse what he or she liked to do before your marriage, like playing certain sports, hiking on certain trails, or reading specific books. Then go do those things together.

- Find a homeless shelter, a children's hospital, or a food bank and offer to volunteer together.

- Write love notes to each other describing what you liked about your spouse when you married and what you like even more about him or her since you have been married. Think about what has gotten better in your relationship and what you've appreciated more and more as time has passed.

- Have a three-legged race, either by yourselves or with other couples.

- Have a day where it's "Take Your Spouse to Work Day."

- Find a creative way to share your love for your spouse in public without embarrassing them.

- Write your own ideas for a great date.

My Ideas and Notes

MY IDEAS AND NOTES

MY IDEAS AND NOTES

MY IDEAS AND NOTES

About the Author

D r. Jerry Cook currently resides in Sacramento, California, with his wife, Sarah, and their three children. Jerry serves as an associate professor in the Department of Family and Consumer Sciences at Sacramento State, where he teaches and has published on parenting, marriage, family relations, adolescence, and adult development. Jerry and Sarah are the authors of *The Parent's Guide to Raising CEO Kids*.